The Archaeology of the Donner Party

Wilbur S. Shepperson Series in History and Humanities

The Archaeology of the Donner Party

DONALD L. HARDESTY

with contributions by

Michael Brodhead : Donald K. Grayson
Susan Lindström : George L. Miller

University of Nevada Press : Reno, Las Vegas

Wilbur S. Shepperson Series in History and
Humanities : Series Editor—Jerome E. Edwards

University of Nevada Press, Reno, Nevada 89557 USA
Copyright © 1997 by University of Nevada Press
All photographs and illustrations © 1997 by Donald L.
Hardesty, unless otherwise noted
All rights reserved
Manufactured in the United States of America
Book design by Carrie Nelson House

Library of Congress Cataloging-in-Publication Data
Hardesty, Donald L., 1941–
    The archaeology of the Donner Party / by Donald
L. Hardesty, with contributions by Michael Brodhead
. . . [et al.].
    p. cm. — (Wilbur S. Shepperson series in history
and humanities)
    Includes bibliographical references and index.
    ISBN 0–87417–290–X (cloth)
    1. Tahoe, Lake, Region (Calif. and Nev.) —
Antiquities. 2. Truckee Region (Calif.)—Antiquities.
3. Excavations (Archaeology)—Tahoe, Lake, Region
(Calif. and Nev.) 4. Excavations (Archaeology)—
California—Truckee Region. 5. Donner Party.
6. Overland journeys to thePacific. I. Brodhead,
Michael J. II. Title. III. Series.
F868.T2H27 1997   96–46836
979.4'38—dc21   CIP

The paper used in this book meets the requirements
of American National Standard for Information
Sciences—Permanence of Paper for Printed Library
Materials, ANSI Z39.48–1984. Binding materials
were selected for strength and durability.

06 05 04 03 02 01 00 99 98 97
5 4 3 2

For Susan and my parents

CONTENTS

FIGURES

TABLES

ACKNOWLEDGMENTS

Many people and organizations contributed to this book. To all, I offer my deepest appreciation. Fritz Riddell, then of the California Department of Parks and Recreation, started me on the archaeological journey into Donner party history by piquing my interest in the Murphy cabin site. The National Geographic Society provided financial assistance with Grant Number 2814-84. Warren Beers and the staff at the Donner Memorial State Park made our lives easier and offered logistical support. I owe a special debt of gratitude to the field school students, field supervisors, staff, and volunteers who worked on the Murphy cabin site: Rick Morris, Susan Lindström, Jack Lagoni, Rolla Queen, Terry Satathite, Mary Panelli, Judy Knokey, Nancy Sikes, Leslie Hill, Grace Fuji, Barbara Sutherland, and Carrie Smith. Many other people contributed to the project. Of these, the following deserve special mention: Sheilagh Brooks and Richard Brooks (University of Nevada, Las Vegas); Amy Dansie (Nevada State Museum), Richard Ahlborn (Smithsonian Institution, National Museum of American History); John Cordine; Martin Rose; William Frank (Huntington Library); the staff of the Bancroft Library; the staff of the California State Library; the staff of the Nevada Historical Society; Michael Brodhead (National Archives); John Foster, Robert Macomber, Norm Wilson, John Rumming, and Lee Motz (California Department of Parks and Recreation); and Jerold M. Lowenstein (University of California School of Medicine, San Francisco).

Richard Markley of the Tahoe National Forest encouraged and made possible the archaeological research at the Alder Creek site. The Tahoe National Forest supported the work with Participating Agreement Number 630154. Carrie Smith (Tahoe National Forest) helped immensely with the logistics of the project. Many field school students, field supervisors, staff, and volunteers worked at the Alder Creek site: Susan Lindström, Arlene Amodei, Gary Bowyer, Tom Cates, Hershel Davis, Mick Sterling, Cynthia Peterson, Sujata Halarnkar, Sherry Reed, Carol Lindsay, John McKenzie, Pharalee Travis-Pawelek, Marvin Pawelek, Sondra James, Jill Jackson, Bonnie Wilson, Jeanne

Albin, Barbara Mackey, Gayle Kromydas, Kellye Vaughn-Gabbert, Janet Shim, Stephanie Wigger, Ava Hahn, Barbara Simmerman, Patee Clark, Donald Griever, Warren McMillan, Florence Rygg, Pat Breckenfeld, Lee Manning, Edith Lasswell, Rick Stafford, Bill Manning, Richard Kraushaar, Ruth Everingham, and Angela Edington.

I also thank Richard Markley and Donna Day (Tahoe National Forest) for organizing and managing the PIT (Passport in Time) metal detector survey of the site in 1993. PIT field supervisors, staff, consultants, and volunteers who worked at the site include Susan Lindström, Leslie Steidl, Deanna Wood, Jan Prior, Sally Metcalf, John Damann, Cheryl Bradford, Priscilla Peterson, Gayle Green, Bruce Steidl, Jack Shipley, Mick Sterling, John McClure, Beppie McClure, Jerry Reddig, Eloise Houston, Chester Zorecki, Dorothy Hildreth, Darryl Nelson, Bob Livesay, Chuck Adams, Nancy Daily, Doris Landberg, Eugene Painter, Rosmarie Mitchell, John Ebel, Hazel Livesay, Jim Hallett, Arlene Amodei, John Roggero, Dolly McClure, Hal Apperson, Frank Williams, Connie Williams, John Tolar, Dorothy Tolar, and Buck Amodei.

Finally, I thank the Nevada Historical Society; the Oregon-California Trails Association; Colonel Charles Graydon and John Corbet for their valuable advice; Norm Wilson; Don Wiggins for allowing me to use his transcription of an emigrant diary; Peter Goin (University of Nevada, Reno) for his two photographs; John Betz (Tahoe National Forest) for his artistic rendering of the reconstructed Murphy cabin; Karen Laramore and Susan Hardesty for the illustrations; C. Lynn Rogers (University of Nevada, Reno) for identifying the buttons; Olive Jones (Canadian Parks Service) for identifying the glass bottles; George Miller (Greiner and Associates) for identifying the ceramics; Glenn Farris (California Department of Parks and Recreation) for identifying the coin from the Isle of Man; Lester Ross for identifying the beads; Harold Klieforth (Desert Research Institute) for climatological information; and Kristin Johnson (Salt Lake Community College), the late Joseph A. King, and Jack Steed, who made me aware of relevant information contained in documents. To those I have overlooked in these acknowledgments, and I'm sure there are many, I offer my apologies and a belated thanks. Finally, I thank my wife, Susan, for her encouragement and patience in bringing this book to a close.

Introduction

In the winter of 1846–1847 nearly half of a group of emigrants traveling overland on their way west to California perished after being trapped by snow in the high elevations of the Sierra Nevada (Figure 1). The survivors lived by eating the boiled hides of their oxen, their pet dogs, wild mice, and anything else edible; finally, they cannibalized their dead. Written accounts of their ordeal appeared shortly afterward, and the tragedy became one of the best-known sagas of the nineteenth-century American West.

Eyewitness accounts of the Donner party's ordeal are not abundant. Perhaps the best known is the diary kept by Patrick Breen, a member of the party, at the mountain camps between November 20, 1846, and March 1, 1847, when he was rescued.[1] James Reed, who was banished from the party after an incident on the Humboldt River, kept a diary relating his experiences with a rescue expedition to the mountain camps conducted between February 21 and March 8, 1847.[2] Other accounts are found in the letters and reminiscences of survivors. In 1891, for example, Virginia Reed Murphy's "Across the Plains in the Donner Party" came out, followed in 1911 by Eliza P. Donner Houghton's *The Expedition of the Donner Party and Its Tragic Fate*.[3] Some diaries written by later emigrants who visited the Donner party's two winter camps not long after they were abandoned contain eyewitness accounts of what remained

Figure 1: The Donner party's route from Independence, Missouri, to Johnson's Ranch in California. Adapted from Map 33, "Overland Tragedies," in Beck and Haase, *Historical Atlas of the American West.*

there. No emigrant accounts mentioning the campsites have been found for 1847 and 1848, however, because most of the overland emigrants went to Oregon and Utah in those years rather than to California. Military records help to fill the gap. A detachment led by General Stephen Watts Kearny passed the campsites on June 22, 1847, on its way east from California to Fort Leavenworth, and its members not only recorded what they saw there but also buried some of the Donner party dead. Most of the surviving emigrant diaries that mention the winter campsites of the Donner party were written by California forty-niners. In 1850, most California emigrants took the Carson River route. Some did travel along the Truckee River route, however, and a few of their diaries mention the campsites.

Secondary histories of the Donner party tragedy began to appear soon after the event. In 1848, Edwin Bryant, who came to California in 1846, published an early account of the Donner party in *What I Saw in California*.[4] Jessy Quinn Thornton, who also came to California with the 1846 emigration, gave what was perhaps the most influential of the early accounts in his *Oregon and California in 1848*,[5] which was published in 1849 and relied mostly on survivor William Eddy's version of the tragedy. In the late 1870s Truckee (California) newspaper editor Charles Fayette McGlashan wrote a series of articles about the event, based on his correspondence and interviews with some of the survivors. He collected and published the newspaper articles in 1879 as *The History of the Donner Party*.[6] McGlashan's book, which changed somewhat in content over the course of its first few editions, remained the authority on the tragedy until George R. Stewart's *Ordeal by Hunger*, published in 1936, supplanted it as the ultimate history of the Donner party. In 1992, Joseph A. King published *Winter of Entrapment*,[7] which gives a somewhat revisionist history of the tragedy and takes Stewart to task for using slanted interpretations and stereotypes, blurring history and fiction, and depending too much on Thornton's account. In addition to these, Bernard DeVoto's *Year of Decision* includes a well-known history of the Donner party, and Dale Morgan's *Overland in 1846* and Kristin Johnson's *Unfortunate Emigrants*, both anthologies containing accounts written by Donner party members, include extensive commentary on the tragedy.[8]

The Donner party rapidly became a symbol of America's westward expansion, and the story soon found its way into fiction, poetry, theater, film, folklore, children's literature, and American popular culture. Bret Harte, for example, used the theme if not the facts of the tragedy as early as 1876 in *Gabriel Conroy*.[9] Later, Hoffman Birney fictionalized but stuck closer to what he viewed as the facts in *Grim Journey* (1934),[10] a novel that relates the story through the eyes of survivor William Eddy, giving the reader a sense of being there and being in command of what actually happened. Vardis Fisher's *The Mothers: An American Saga of Courage* (1943), Julia Cooley Altrocchi's *Snow-Covered Wagons, a Pioneer Epic* (1936), Ruth Whitman's *A Woman's Journey* (1985), and Jeanette Gould Maino's *Left Hand Turn: A Story of the Donner Party Women* (1987) are but a few of the other fictionalized and dramatized versions of the tragedy.[11]

How We Know About the Donner Party Tragedy

David Lowenthal says that "the past is a foreign country" through which we travel along the routes of memory, history, and relics.[12] Our knowledge of the past comes from the interconnections among these routes. "Memory, history, and relics offer routes to the past best traversed in combination," he claims. "Each route requires the others for the journey to be significant and credible. Relics trigger recollection, which history affirms and extends backward in time. History in isolation is barren and lifeless; relics mean only what history and memory convey. Indeed, many artifacts originated as memorial or historical witnesses. Significant apprehension of the past demands engagement with previous experience, one's own and others', along all three routes."[13] Combining these sources of information, which are normally independent of one another, enhances our awareness of the past not only by expanding our "objective" knowledge, but also by giving us a better understanding of how the present influences our understanding, knowledge, and interpretation of the past. Each source of historical evidence, however, has intrinsic weaknesses and strengths, and the kinds of historical evidence that can be brought to bear on a particular case vary enormously. Sometimes, for example, written accounts of an event simply do not exist. Obviously, nonliterate people do not keep diaries or other written accounts of their lives. The passage of time finally removes oral testimony as a source of firsthand information about the past. And in some instances, history has preserved no relics of the past.

Personal motives—why individuals do what they do, or did what they did—reside in and must be interpreted from written accounts and memory; material things, no matter how complete and well preserved, provide no clues to the motives of individuals. Of course, the historical reconstruction of motives also is the most susceptible to "presentism," interpreting the past through the colored glasses of what we in the present think to be reasonable motives and courses of action.[14]

The Testimony of the Spade

The existing Donner party histories rely almost exclusively on the evidence contained in written accounts, including contemporary letters and journals kept by party members and rescue parties, and later recollections of the survivors. When C. F. McGlashan wrote the first history of the Donner party tragedy in 1879, for example, he relied largely on the memories of the survivors. Archaeologist Geoffrey Bibby's now-classic popular book *The Testimony of the Spade* suggests another method of finding information that can be used to interpret the past: archaeology.[15] Of course, the use of archaeology to find artifacts and other material remains as a source of information about the past is not particularly new to studies of the Donner party. As early as the 1870s, C. F. McGlashan and some of the survivors of the tragedy dug into the remains of two of the mountain cabins where some members of the party had lived during the winter of 1846–1847. Fragments of "old porcelain and china-ware . . . readily distinguished by painted flowers, or unique designs enameled in red, blue, or purple colors" were unearthed at a depth of one to six inches in the floor of the Breen cabin.[16] A cooper's inshave, an iron wagon hammer, and a whetstone with the initials "JFR" (James Frazier Reed), along with round-headed pins and a tin box once containing hemlock, were dug up at the Graves-Reed cabin in 1879.[17] Other artifacts dug up at the cabins included glass tableware, buttons, fishhooks, gunflints, mirrors, and "bolts, nails, screws, nuts, chains, and portions of wagon irons."[18] In *Ordeal by Hunger*, George R. Stewart mentions that on November 12, 1935, he "did some excavation at [the site of the Alder Creek camp, where the George and Jacob Donner families had been trapped], finding at two places layers of charcoal deposits about four inches below the present ground-level."[19]

Several recent attempts have been made to use physical remains to study the saga of the Donner party. Jack and Richard Steed, for example, dug at the site of the main house at Johnson's Ranch, the place in the Sierra Nevada foothills where the Donner party rescue attempts were launched, and reported the results in *The Donner Party Rescue Site, Johnson's Ranch on Bear River*.[20] Although their report gives no detailed description of the excavation or the artifacts found at the site, it does include photographs and a brief artifact list. The artifacts, which appear to be typical of the period, include clay tobacco pipes, kitchen and table utensils (spoons, knives, and forks), door hinges, a military eagle buckle, a brass patch box from an 1841 "Mississippi" rifle, musket balls, suspender clasps, harness buckles, tent grommets, a powder flask, a compass, percussion caps, animal shoes (ox, mule, and horse), cut and hand-made nails, a double-set rifle trigger, buttons, jewelry, a pocket knife, shell-edged and sprig-decorated English ceramic tableware, and an oil lamp base with wick holder.[21]

In *Excavation of the Donner-Reed Wagons*, Bruce Hawkins and David Madsen of the Utah State Historical Society report on the 1986 excavation of the remains of several wagons thought to have been abandoned by the Donner party in the mud flats of the Great Salt Lake Desert.[22] Archaeological traces of the wagons include "wagon wheel ruts, identifiable stains of metal wagon parts such as wheels, wooden wagon parts, extensive concentration of charcoal, animal remains, and scattering of small early to mid-nineteenth century artifacts."[23] A wagon site with unusually wide wheel tracks impressed into the clay playa and associated with the remains of an abandoned cache of goods, both covered by the same sand dune, may be the place where James F. Reed's "Pioneer Palace" was abandoned for a time; none of the other wagon sites, however, could be identified precisely. The 184 identifiable artifacts recovered from the Reed wagon site are mostly fragments of firearms (including musket balls, percussion caps, and gunflints), tack and animal equipment, wagon parts, and clothing. A few household artifacts (food and toiletry containers such as glass medicine bottle fragments, a glazed stoneware bottle or jug handle, an ink bottle, and a hotel china salt dish) and hand tools (e.g., augers and grass hooks) also are represented in the assemblage. Except for a single military button, personal items such as jewelry and tobacco pipes are missing entirely.

In 1984 the University of Nevada, Reno (UNR) began archaeological studies

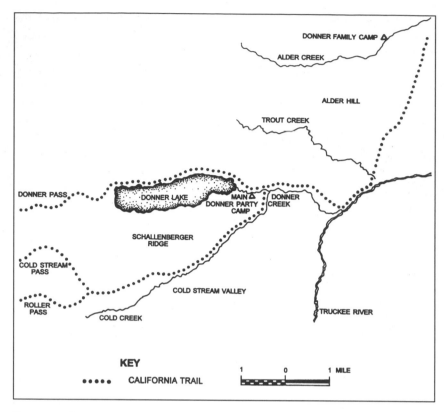

Figure 2: The two Donner party mountain camps. Adapted from map by Clyde H. Welsh in consort with Don Buck, in Hardesty, "Donner Party Archaeology," p. 20.

of the two Donner mountain camps near what is now Truckee, California (Figure 2). The first excavation took place at the site of the Murphy cabin.[24] Although C. F. McGlashan, Donner party survivors, and members of the Truckee community dug into the other two cabins in 1879, they left the Murphy cabin untouched, noting that the "marsh grass . . . firmly resists either shovel or spade."[25] What happened to the other lake cabins after 1879 is uncertain. The Graves-Reed cabin may have been destroyed during the construction of, or buried by, Interstate 80. McGlashan stated in 1920 that workmen "removed all traces of the floor, the fireplace, and even the stump" of the Breen cabin in 1909 during construction of the Pioneer Monument at what is now Donner Memorial State Park.[26] But C. W. Chapman, chairman of the Donner Memorial Committee, which constructed the monument, announced in the same year that the cabin stood in another place altogether.[27]

In fact, the location of the Murphy cabin was still in question when the UNR group began its excavation. In 1879, Donner party survivors had pointed out to McGlashan the large granite boulder against which the cabin had been built.

Today, a bronze plaque, placed in the early twentieth century, marks the boulder, which is a key attraction of Donner Memorial State Park. The location of the cabin (based almost entirely on oral tradition) remained in dispute until the 1984 and 1985 excavations confirmed that the marked boulder is indeed the correct site of the Murphy cabin. The excavators found gunflints, lead balls, ceramic tableware, table utensils, glass bottle fragments, buttons, jewelry, a religious medal, shoe parts, clay tobacco pipes, and hardware, as well as burned bone, charcoal and ash deposits, and charred log fragments.

In 1990 the University of Nevada, Reno, began to excavate the reputed site of the other mountain camp, on Alder Creek, several miles away from the lake.[28] C. F. McGlashan first located the site in 1879 with the help of some Donner party survivors and rescue party members. Located once again in the 1920s, the site was disputed by some because of its distance from the main overland trail normally used by emigrants. The excavators, however, found archaeological evidence confirming McGlashan's identification, including percussion caps, lead balls, ceramic tableware, table utensils, glass bottle fragments, buttons, two coins, a military emblem, hand tools, wagon hardware, and animal equipage. The artifacts resembled those found at the Murphy cabin site in many ways but differed in some. Ceramic tableware, for example, was much more abundant at Alder Creek. Additional archaeological research in 1992 and 1993 added to our knowledge of the camp where the George and Jacob Donner families and their entourage lived.

Archaeology to the Rescue

If archaeology is indeed another pathway to understanding the Donner party tragedy, what specific questions can it answer? Let us consider some of these. Probably the most important question centers on the location of the Alder Creek camp. Unlike the lake camp, the camp on Alder Creek is not well documented in written accounts. Tamsen Donner was said to have kept a diary, but it has never been found. Brief eyewitness glimpses of the camp appear in James Reed's diary and in the reminiscences of Eliza Donner Houghton, Elitha Donner Wilder, and Jean Baptiste Trudeau. In 1879 C. F. McGlashan first visited the site with Nicholas Clark, a member of the second relief party who had stayed for a while at the camp, and later returned with W. C. Graves. He placed the camp on Alder Creek about a mile north of the most commonly used branch of the emigrant trail. Peter M. Weddell, a San Jose schoolteacher, re-marked the site in the 1920s.

How many shelters were there, and how far apart were they? The actual layout of the Alder Creek camp is unknown except in a very general way. The written accounts mention only two shelters, but the size and composition of the Donner family group make more seem likely. Archaeology is uniquely qualified to uncover and help us reconstruct the architectural details of the cabins and shelters at the two mountain camps.

Did cannibalism actually occur? It is commonly believed that some members of the Donner party survived by eating their dead. Jessy Quinn Thornton's early history, for example, the first comprehensive account of the tragedy, and based on interviews with survivors, includes numerous references to cannibalism. In addition, some personal accounts by survivors and relief party members mention cannibalism. The only directly observable physical evidence of cannibalism available to us, however, comes from human bone with cut marks. Recent studies of the skeletal remains of Alferd Packer's partner in Colorado, for example, another famous case of cannibalism on the western frontier, show such marks. Perhaps excavation of the Murphy cabin site, the reputed location of a mass grave of Donner party remains, can answer the question once and for all.

And what about the material possessions carried by the Donner party to the two mountain camps? In many ways the company's baggage is a time capsule reflecting the lifeways of American consumers on the eve of the industrial revolution. Their possessions also say something about the material things the party members believed to be most important. All but the most valuable items were left behind in caches along the trail. Finally, the testimony of the spade will shed light on the everyday life of the people who lived in the two mountain camps through physical evidence that is completely independent of written accounts and oral testimony.

The following chapters contain vignettes of the two Donner party mountain camps created by combining archaeological, documentary, and other evidence. Chapter 1 tells the story of the Donner party. Chapter 2, written by historian Michael Brodhead of the National Archives, places the Donner party in the larger context of the 1846 overland migration, focusing on the emigrants' motivation. The next two chapters describe the archaeological investigations at the two mountain camps. Chapter 3, written with archaeologist Susan Lindström, reconstructs the Murphy cabin, one of the three cabins at the lake camp. Chapter 4 describes what we know about the Alder Creek camp and the Donner families' shelters there. Chapter 5 examines the material culture of the Donner party as viewed through written accounts and archaeological evidence. Finally, Chapter 6 describes new directions in Donner party research.

1 : The Donner Party Saga

The opening of the California Trail by the Bartleson-Bidwell party in 1841 launched an episode of cross-country emigration unparalleled in American history. In the years between 1840 and 1860, an estimated 300,000 emigrants journeyed overland to what is now California, Oregon, and Utah.[1] Despite the large number of emigrants who took the overland route and the many hardships they faced along the way, only a few groups met with real disaster—the Donner party in 1846–1847, the Jayhawker party in Death Valley in 1849, and the Willie handcart party in 1856 are the best known.[2] Of these, the Donner party tragedy exemplifies particularly well both the myth and the reality of the overland emigrant experience. The events that took place in the Sierra Nevada during the winter of 1846–1847 have become an icon of the American westward movement.

George Donner, a prosperous sixty-two-year-old farmer from Illinois who had moved five times before, was the elected captain of the party. He started the journey with his sixty-five-year-old brother Jacob and James Frazier Reed, age forty-five, an ambitious and well-off furniture maker. The three families—thirty-two people and nine wagons in all—left Springfield, Illinois, on April 16, 1846. Sometime during the second week in May, they arrived in Independence, Missouri, the eastern terminus of the California Trail. There they joined 2,700 other emigrants and five hundred wagons that had aggregated for the trip west. The wagons left Independence without much coherence but later formed into more organized parties. Reed and the Donners joined one of these, a company of forty-nine wagons under the captainship of Colonel William "Owl" Russell, somewhere in the vicinity of the Kansas River on May 20, 1846. They arrived at Fort Laramie, in what is now Wyoming, toward the end of June without event—although Mrs. Reed's mother, Sarah Keyes, died of old age on the way—and continued on their journey to the Rocky Mountains.

On July 19, 1846, the Russell party reached the Little Sandy River just beyond South Pass, Wyoming, and the Continental Divide. Here, the emigrants had to decide whether to follow the more established trail or take the new shortcut advocated by California promoter Lansford Hastings in his popular 1845 emigrant guidebook. The shortcut went past Fort Bridger, Wyoming, down through the Wasatch Mountains, and across the Great Salt Lake Desert to the Humboldt River, where it rejoined the main California Trail. For the first few years after the California Trail was opened, overland emigrants hired guides to take them the rest of the way. By 1846, however, as historian John Unruh notes, that had changed: "By now the trails were clearly visible, informative letters from previous overlanders had been published and otherwise widely circulated, and guidebooks were also available. Many emigrants that year carried Lansford Hastings's volume."[3] The Donners and the Reeds did. They convinced themselves that the shortcut would save time and disregarded the advice offered at Fort Laramie by mountain man James Clyman, who had served with Reed in the Black Hawk War and had just completed a trip with Hastings eastward from California along the shortcut.[4]

Most of the Russell company opted conservatively for the well-marked trail to Oregon, but some split off from the main group and moved toward Fort Bridger with the intention of taking the Hastings cutoff. Among them were the nine wagons of the Donner and Reed families along with eleven other wagons. They were among the last of those traveling in the great emigration of 1846 to leave the Little Sandy. The group elected George Donner as its captain, although the aristocratic James Reed appears to have been more influential. After reaching Fort Bridger, the party stayed for a short time, lost some members but added several others, and then continued toward the Hastings cutoff on July 31, 1846. The company reached its maximum size—eighty-seven people traveling in twenty-two wagons—after the Franklin Graves family and their teamster, John Snyder, caught up with them in the Wasatch Mountains. The trip through the Wasatch Mountains proved to be much more strenuous than any of the party expected. Instead of taking the canyon route marked by Hastings, the company opted to cut a new trail to the crest of the mountains—the trail followed the next year by Brigham Young and his Mormon pioneers. The new route required cutting a path through miles of narrow and heavily wooded canyons with hand axes, an exhausting ordeal that may have played an important role in bringing about the early deaths of the adult males after the party became trapped in the high elevations of the Sierra Nevada. The trek through the Wasatch took at least eighteen days, much longer than expected, and it was not until August 22, 1846, that the company finally reached the Great Salt Lake Valley. They had lost precious time. The group's diverse ethnic, national, and cultural composition, together with clashing personalities, fragmented the party. Small cliques, such as the wagons of the Donner family, traveled separately, spreading the wagon train out for miles along the trail. The party's lack of social cohesion also had much to do with the difficulties that arose on the way to California.

The trip across the valley and the salt flats south of the lake was another great ordeal. Several wagons had to be abandoned on the Great Salt Lake Desert, including the large "Pioneer Palace" of James Reed (see chapter 5), which was later recovered. On September 4, 1846, the company finally reached Pilot Peak on the western edge of the desert, set up camp, and went back to retrieve the cattle and wagons they had lost or abandoned in the desert. More time was lost and more dissension set in. One member of the group, Luke Halloran, died of illness, the first death recorded since the party had left Fort Bridger. Only eighteen wagons remained, and supplies were running very low. Charles Stanton and William McCutchen volunteered to go ahead to Sutter's Fort in California to bring back some desperately needed food.

After spending a week in the Pilot Peak camp, the company continued on, finally reaching the main California Trail at the Humboldt River in what is now central Nevada on September 26. Another member of the party died while the group was traveling down the Humboldt. During a squabble on October 4, James Reed killed John Snyder, the driver of one of the Graves family's wagons, and was banished from the party. Reed's family remained with the party, but Walter Herron, his teamster, joined him in exile. They managed to reach Sutter's Fort on October 28, and Reed later helped to rescue the survivors of the Donner party in the Sierra Nevada. With Reed gone, the company rapidly lost whatever social cohesion had remained and began to fall apart. During the next two weeks, as the group continued the trek to the Humboldt Sink and crossed the Forty-Mile Desert to the Truckee River Canyon, two more members of the party died: a Mr. Hardkoop from Belgium and Jacob Wolfinger—the former abandoned and the latter apparently killed by other members of the party. More wagons and possessions had to be abandoned along the way. A letter written by twelve-year-old Virginia Reed to her cousin in Springfield on May 16, 1847, describes what happened to her family:

in 2 or 3 days after pa [James Reed] left we had to cash [cache] our wagon and take Mr. Graves wagon and cash some more of our things. Well we went on that way a while and then we had to get Mr eddies wagon we went on that way a while and then we had to cash all our close [clothes] except a change or 2 and put them in Mr. Bri [Breens] Wagon and Thomas and James rode the other 2 horses and the rest of us had to walk. we went on that way a While and we come to a nother long drive of 40 miles [the Forty-Mile Desert] and then we went with Mr. Donner We had to walk all the time we was a traveling up the truckee river.[5]

The party reached the Truckee River in mid-October with only fourteen wagons. Three days later they encountered Charles Stanton, who was returning from Sutter's Fort in the company of Luis and Salvador,[6] two of Sutter's Indian employees, with seven pack mules carrying much-needed food. William McCutchen, who had traveled to the fort with Stanton, was too ill to make the return trip.

Sometime during the third week of October, the company arrived in the Truckee Meadows (now Reno) at the base of the Sierra Nevada and stayed for several days before attempting to cross the mountains into California. The written records do not indicate exactly where they camped. Most later emigrant parties, however, left the Truckee River near the present-day Reno-Sparks sewage treatment plant and traveled for about two miles along the eastern edge of the meadow before turning west at the base of Rattlesnake Mountain, camping anywhere along that stretch. The Donner party probably camped there as well. Archaeological remains of emigrant camps have been reported from this area, but the construction of modern housing developments destroyed all traces of them before a systematic study could take place. During their stay in the Truckee Meadows, the group lost another member, William Pike, to the accidental discharge of a firearm. They stayed about a week in the Truckee Meadows—in retrospect probably much too long, but understandable given the poor health and social condition of the emigrants and their draft animals— and finally left in three separate groups. The Donner family contingent was the last to begin the trek up the Truckee River Canyon toward the mountains. The weather failed at the same time. An early winter storm began in the mountains on October 28 and continued with only short breaks until November 11.

Some accounts of the Donner party's trip up the canyon suggest conflict between the emigrants and local Indians. Years later, for example, Sarah Winnemucca Hopkins related a story about the Donner party burning her people's winter caches:

Well, while we were in the mountains hiding, the people that my grandfather called our white brothers came along to where our winter supplies were. They set everything we had left on fire. It was a fearful sight. It was all we had for the winter, and it was all burnt during that night. My father took some of his men during the night to try and save some of it, but they could not; it had burnt down before they got there.

These were the last white men that came along that fall. My people talked fearfully that winter about those they called our white brothers. My people said they had something like awful thunder and lightning [firearms], and with that they killed everything in sight.

This whole band of white people perished in the mountains, for it was too late to cross them. We could have saved them, only my people were afraid of them. We never knew who they were, or where they came from. So, poor things, they must have suffered fearfully, for they all starved there. The snow was too deep.[7]

The first two parties, about two-thirds of the company, reached what is now Donner Lake on October 31 (Figure 3). They tried to continue, but deep snow and a winter storm forced them to turn back to the lake. Here, after another failed attempt to cross the mountains, they set up what they expected to be a temporary camp on November 4 and waited.

The Donner family entourage, the last group to leave the Truckee Meadows and further delayed by a broken wagon axle on the trail, found themselves trapped by the same winter storm. Years later, Elitha C. Donner Wilder related that part of the story to her sister Eliza:

We were 12 to 15 miles from the place where we camped for the winter coming down a long sliding hill, father was driving, you [Eliza Donner Houghton] and Georgia [Donner] were in the wagon, your mother and Frances were walking ahead when near the bottom the axel of the fore wheel broke and the wagon tipped down tumbling everything over you two children. Father and Uncle Jake rushed to get you out. Georgia was soon drawn out through the opening at the back, but you were out of sight and father feared that you were smothered for you did not answer his anxious call. Uncle kept right on pulling things out until he came to you.[8]

George Donner severely cut his hand while preparing a new axle for the wagon. The cut became infected and made him an invalid who had to be cared for by his wife and family. The Donner family set up a camp near what is now Alder Creek, about five miles northeast of the lake camp. Trapped by deep snow, the two groups lived in their mountain camps for much of the winter. No outsider reached either camp for nearly four months. Some information about what went on during this time, however, is recorded in a diary kept by Patrick Breen between November 20, 1846, and March 1, 1847. On December 15,

Figure 3: Donner Lake, looking southeast. The site of the Donner party lake camp is at the east end of the lake (left).

1846, the first death in the mountain camps occurred when Baylis Williams, one of the Reed family's servants, died of starvation and exposure. More deaths rapidly followed. Of the eighty-one people trapped in the camps, only forty-eight were still alive when the last survivor left the mountain camps on April 21, 1847, and reached safety four days later (see Table 1).

The company did not sit docilely in the mountains all winter without trying to get out, of course. There were three attempts to escape, and there were also attempts from outside to rescue the stranded emigrants. The first rescue effort failed to get off the ground. On reaching Sutter's Fort, James Reed tried to organize a rescue expedition. He and William McCutchen, now recovered from the illness that had prevented him from returning with Charles Stanton and the food, left the fort on October 31 with the intention of bringing aid to the party. Unfortunately, the same early winter storm that forced the Donner party into the mountain camps doomed that attempt. Not until the end of February was Reed able to organize a successful rescue. In the meantime, he participated in the now-raging Mexican American War.

What happened to the first attempt by the survivors to escape from their mountain entrapment is recorded in Patrick Breen's November 23 diary entry: "the Expedition across the mountains returned after an unsuccsful [*sic*] attempt."[9] The second attempt by the stranded company to escape the mountain camps resulted in a terrible tragedy. On December 16, seventeen members of the group left the lake camp on snowshoes fashioned out of oxbows and rawhide. Two turned back after one day. The rest, ten men and five women, soon lost the trail over the mountains. On January 18, a month later, the seven survivors of the "Forlorn Hope," the name often given to the snowshoe party, finally arrived at Johnson's Ranch in Bear Valley, seventy miles away. All five of the women and two of the men survived the ordeal. The snowshoers seem to have been the first members of the Donner party to cannibalize their dead. Mrs. James Reed led the third escape party on January 4, but it too was forced to turn back after several days. Patrick Breen's January 8 entry notes that "Mrs. Reid [sic] & company came back this mor[n]ing could not find their way on the other side of the mountain."[10]

In the meantime, back at the mountain camps, five more members of the stranded company, all males, had perished from exposure and starvation by the end of December. Death had taken two others, also males, by the end of January. No outsider reached the camps until February 18, when the first relief party arrived at the lake camp. Nearly four months had passed since the Donner party had been trapped in the mountains. On February 22, the seven rescuers left the two mountain camps with twenty-three members of the Donner party, most of them children. Two of the Reed children were unable to continue and soon returned to the lake camp, but the rest of the group reached the head of Bear Valley on February 27 and continued on to Johnson's Ranch. During the trip, three more members of the Donner party died, including John Denton, an Englishman who had traveled with the George Donner family.

The second relief party was not far behind the first. Reed and McCutchen organized the expedition and left Johnson's Ranch on February 22. They met the first relief party on its way back at the head of Bear Valley and reached the lake on March 1. The second relief party found twenty-eight people still alive at the two mountain camps. An entry in Patrick Breen's diary and observations made by the rescuers suggest that cannibalism had taken place at both camps. Breen wrote in his diary on February 26 that "Mrs. Murphy said here yesterday that [she] thought she would commence on Milt. [Elliott] and eat him. I dont [think] that she has done so yet, it is distressing. The Donnos [Donners] told the California folks [the first relief] that they [would] commence to eat the dead people 4 days ago, if they did not succeed that day or next in finding their cattle then under ten or twelve feet of snow." The second relief party found the mutilated remains of Milt Elliott in the Murphy cabin. They also mentioned finding evidence of cannibalism at the Alder Creek camp.

The second relief party left the lake on March 3 with seventeen of the survivors. On the way back they were caught by a large winter storm and had to leave thirteen people behind in a temporary camp, soon to be known as "Starved Camp." When the rest of Reed's party reached Bear Valley a few days later, the third relief party was organized. They finally found the stranded emigrants at Starved Camp in mid-March; three had died, and the rest had sur-

Table 1: Donner Party Roster

Name	Age[1]	Comment
Antonio (Antoine)	[23]	Died in mountains
Breen, Edward	13	
Breen, James	5	
Breen, John	14	
Breen, Margaret Isabella	1	
Breen, Margaret Bulger	40	
Breen, Patrick	51	
Breen, Patrick Jr.	9	
Breen, Peter	3	
Breen, Simon	8	
Burger, Charles	[30]	Died in mountains
Denton, John	[28]	
Dolan, Patrick	35	Died in mountains
Donner, Elitha	14	
Donner, Eliza	3	
Donner, Elizabeth	[45]	Died in mountains
Donner, Frances	6	
Donner, George	[62]	Died in mountains
Donner, George Jr.	9	
Donner, Georgia	4	
Donner, Isaac	[5]	Died in mountains
Donner, Jacob	[65]	Died in mountains
Donner, Leanna	12	
Donner, Lewis	3	Died in mountains
Donner, Mary	7	
Donner, Samuel	4	Died in mountains
Donner, Tamsen	[44]	Died in mountains
Eddy, Eleanor	[25]	Died in mountains
Eddy, James	3	Died in mountains
Eddy, Margaret	1	Died in mountains
Eddy, William	[28]	
Elliott, Milford (Milt)	[28]	Died in mountains
Fosdick, Jay	[23]	Died in mountains
Fosdick, Sarah	21	
Foster, George	4	Died in mountains
Foster, Sarah	19	
Foster, William	[30]	
Graves, Eleanor	14	
Graves, Elizabeth	1	
Graves, Elizabeth Cooper	47	Died in mountains
Graves, Franklin	[57]	Died in mountains

continued

Name	Age[1]	Comment
Graves, Franklin Jr.	[5]	Died in mountains
Graves, Jonathan	[7]	
Graves, Lovina	12	
Graves, Mary Ann	19	
Graves, Nancy	9	
Graves, William	7	
Halloran, Luke	[25]	Died on trail
Hardcoop	[60]	Died on trail
Herron, Walter	[27]	
Hook, Solomon	14	
Hook, William	12	Died in mountains
James, Noah	[20]	
Keseberg, Ada	3	Died in mountains
Keseberg, Lewis (Louis)	32	
Keseberg, Lewis (Louis) Jr.	1	Died in mountains
Keseberg, Philippine	23	
Luis[2]	[?]	Died in mountains
McCutchen, Amanda	[25]	
McCutchen, Harriet	1	Died in mountains
McCutchen, William	[30]	
Murphy, John Landrum	16	Died in mountains
Murphy, Lavina (Levinah)	36	Died in mountains
Murphy, Lemuel	12	Died in mountains
Murphy, Mary	14	
Murphy, Simon	8	
Murphy, William	10	
Pike, Catherine	1	Died in mountains
Pike, Harriet	18	
Pike, Naomi	2	
Pike, William M.	[25]	Died on trail
Reed, James	45	
Reed, James Jr.	6	
Reed, Margaret	[32]	
Reed, Martha (Patty)	9	
Reed, Thomas	4	
Reed, Virginia	13	
Reinhardt, Joseph	[30]	Died in mountains
Salvador[2]	[?]	Died in mountains
Shoemaker, Samuel	[25]	Died in mountains
Smith, James	[25]	Died in mountains
Snyder, John	[25]	Died on trail

continued

Name	Age[1]	Comment
Spitzer, Augustus	[30]	Died in mountains
Stanton, Charles	[35]	Died in mountains
Trudeau, Jean (John) Baptiste	16	
Williams, Baylis	[25]	Died in mountains
Williams, Eliza	31	
Wolfinger	[?]	Died on trail
Wolfinger, Doris	[20?]	

Source: Based on Johnson, *Unfortunate Emigrants*, 294–298.

1. Following Johnson, the ages are based on the timeline of July 31, 1846, the date the Donner party started on the Hastings cutoff. The ages in brackets are estimates.

2. Sutter's Fort employees carrying supplies who reached the Donner party on the Truckee River and were trapped with the party in the mountains.

vived by cannibalizing the dead. The third group of rescuers continued on to the lake, where they found only ten people still alive in the two mountain camps—seven in Murphy's cabin and three at the Donner family camp. The third relief party left the lake on March 13 with four of the surviving children, Jean Baptiste Trudeau, and Nicholas Clark, a member of the second relief party who had remained behind to care for the dying George Donner. Only five people remained behind in the mountain camps.

A month passed before the fourth relief party reached the camps (one expedition had failed to get beyond Bear Valley). In any case, rescue was no longer such an urgent matter. No one expected George Donner, Sammie Donner, or Mrs. Murphy to be alive; Tamsen Donner had turned down two opportunities to come out; and no one cared about Lewis Keseberg, who already had been publicized as a cannibal. On the other hand, the Donner party had left behind enough of their material possessions to make it worthwhile to mount a salvage expedition to the mountain camps, and that was the fourth rescue party's focus. The expedition left Johnson's Ranch on April 13 and arrived at the lake on April 17. Led by mountain man William O. "Le Gros" Fallon, the expedition found only Lewis Keseberg alive. Of the other four, only George Donner's body at Alder Creek was found. The fourth relief party left with Lewis Keseberg on April 21, reached the upper end of Bear Valley on April 22, and arrived at Johnson's Ranch on April 25, 1847. The Donner party's ordeal was finally over. Forty-eight members of the company had survived.

2 : The Donner Party and Overland Emigration, 1840–1860

MICHAEL BRODHEAD

Until they became hopelessly trapped in the winter snows of the Sierra Nevada, the members of the Donner party were in most respects typical of overland travelers in the antebellum years. In terms of motives, composition, equipment, itinerary, and trail experiences, the Donner company was remarkably similar to countless other groups who headed for California and Oregon in the decades before the Civil War.[1]

In some notable ways, however, the Donner party differed from most other migrating companies of the period. At that time, the goal of most Americans seeking homes beyond the Mississippi was the Oregon country. The route to California, the Donner party's destination, was far less well defined than the road to the Pacific Northwest in the pre–gold rush era, and California itself was still in Mexican hands when the party began its journey. Although possession of Oregon was disputed between the United States and Great Britain, the question was settled peaceably by 1847; it took a war with Mexico to make California and other northern Mexican provinces American property. Both on the trail and at its end, then, the outlook was less certain for Americans bound for California in 1846 than it was for those seeking to settle in Oregon.

The Donner group also contained a larger than usual percentage of elderly persons and children, and a correspondingly smaller component of young adult males ("fighting men," in the parlance of the overlanders). The relative lack of mature, sturdy adults—women as well as men—made the adversities of the fatal last leg of the journey even more difficult to surmount.

Apart from these differences, to study the Donner party is to study a highly representative body of emigrants. In the years from 1840 to 1848, an estimated 11,512 Americans reached Oregon, and only 2,735 came to California. But in 1846, the year the Donners and their companions set out, the number of California-bound emigrants exceeded the number of those going to Oregon, 1,500 to 1,200.[2]

What explains the growing interest in Mexican California in the years before the discovery of gold in 1848? Probably the greatest single influence was John C. Frémont's report on his explorations of 1843–1844, although the expansionist rhetoric of Frémont's father-in-law, Senator Thomas Hart Benton, the descriptions of California found in Richard Henry Dana's *Two Years before the Mast* (1840), and Lansford W. Hastings's *Emigrants' Guide to Oregon and California* (1845) also contributed to the interest in California and other provinces of northern Mexico. Newspapers, such as the *Sangamo Journal* of Springfield, Illinois—the home community of the Donner and Reed families—likewise advocated American settlement of the Pacific Coast. The Donners and other prospective emigrant families in the Springfield vicinity had read the works of Frémont and Hastings.[3] Other early travel accounts that helped to foster migration to California included Thomas Jefferson Farnham's *Travels in the California and Scenes in the Pacific Ocean* (1844) and John M. Shively's *Route and Distances to Oregon and California* (1846). These and other voices spoke seductively of a lush, idyllic land ready for settlement by energetic Americans—and perhaps ripe to be plucked from Mexico's tenuous hold.

The motives of those emigrating to California before the gold rush of 1849 varied from one individual to another, of course.[4] The majority were farmers, as were most Americans of that period, who hoped to acquire grants of California's fertile acreage. In a newspaper advertisement, George Donner assured prospective members of his party, "You can have as much land as you want without costing you anything. The government of California gives large tracts of land to persons who have to move there."[5] En route to California, Donner's observant wife, Tamsen, found the prairie between the Blue and Platte Rivers "beautiful beyond description" and "so suitable for cultivation." But this area would not become available to emigrants until 1854. Meanwhile, the even more pleasing lands of California beckoned.

Also among the principal benefits enticing Americans to California was the reputedly healthful climate. Edwin Bryant, who traveled much of the way in the same group as the Donners, was emphatic on this point. "The general reason assigned for emigration to the Pacific, by those from the frontier settlements of Illinois and Missouri," he said, was "the extreme unhealthiness of those districts," whose inhabitants regularly suffered from ague and "congestive fever." The wife of James F. Reed, a major figure in the Donner party, suffered from "sick headaches," and the restoration of her health and that of her invalid mother was a factor in Reed's decision to emigrate to California. Consumptive Luke Halloran, another member of the Donner party, hoped that the new climate would repair his shattered constitution.[6]

J. Quinn Thornton, another of those who traveled part of the distance with the Donners and Reeds, also suffered from ill health, as did his wife. He too wrote that California's lands and healthful climate were powerful magnets, but he also pointed out other reasons given by the emigrants. Some were debtors hoping to restore their finances. For others it was "love of change" and the "spirit of enterprise and adventure." And some, Thornton believed, "knew not exactly why they were thus upon the road."[7]

Momentum seems to have been the main force impelling Charles T. Stanton westward. Writing to his brother from Independence, Missouri, where he had joined the Donners, he confessed that he had come there from Chicago without plans to go farther west, "but traveling had such an agreeable effect on me and having once got afloat that I have found it as hard to stop myself from going as I did in the first place to set myself in motion." Stanton also hoped that the trip and its excitement might "restore some of my dormant energies which have been so long asleep."[8]

Motive alone could not take an emigrant to California or Oregon; it was essential to have the means both to make the journey and to become settled when the destination was reached. Historians have long since exploded the myth that poor Americans could simply head west and improve their fortunes, and that the frontier was a "safety valve" in hard times—as the 1840s were. Eliza Donner Houghton, daughter of George and Tamsen Donner, recalled much interest in California emigration in Sangamon County in 1846, "and had it not been for the widespread financial depression of that year, a large number would have gone from the vicinity. The great cost of equipment, however, kept back many who desired to make the long journey."[9]

George Donner and his brother Jacob were substantial Sangamon County farmers who took their families to California with expectations of bettering their already good lot. James F. Reed was an ambitious and well-off furniture manufacturer with visions of a business paradise. Others who attached themselves to the Donner party along the trail were at least comfortably fixed; for example, Patrick Breen and his family owned a farm near Keokuk, Iowa, as did Breen's fellow Irishman Patrick Dolan.[10] Franklin Ward Graves and his family, also of Illinois, traveled with a considerable amount of hard currency, as did Luke Halloran and the Donners themselves. Francis Parkman, a young Boston patrician who also went overland in 1846, observed that "many of the emigrants, especially those bound for California, were persons of wealth and standing."[11]

Of course, a great many overlanders were not so well fixed. The advertisement taken out by George Donner in the *Sangamo Journal* of March 26, 1846, illustrates one means by which the impecunious could travel to the Pacific: "Who wants to go to California without costing them anything? As many as eight young men, of good character who can drive an ox team, will be accommodated by gentlemen who will leave this vicinity about the first of April. . . . The first suitable persons who apply will be engaged."[12] Among those who traveled as hired hands of the Donners, Reeds, and Graveses were Milford Elliott, Walter Herron, Noah James, Samuel Shoemaker, James Smith, John Snyder, the New Mexicans Jean Baptiste Trudeau ("Trubode") and Antonio, and Baylis Williams and his sister Eliza.

The Donner party was typical of other emigrant groups of the pre–Civil War era not only in its socioeconomic diversity but also in its varied ethnic character. Most of the immigrants to America in the first half of the nineteenth century came from the British Isles and northern Europe. The foreign-born members of the Donner party certainly reflect this pattern. James Reed was born in northern Ireland and may have been partly of Polish descent. Patrick Breen and his wife, Margaret, were Irish-born Catholics who had come to Iowa via Canada. Their neighbor, Patrick Dolan, was also born in Ireland. John Denton was a native of England. Hardkoop came from Belgium. Charles Burger, Lewis and Philippine Keseberg, Joseph Reinhardt, Augustus Spitzer, and the Wolfinger family were German speakers. The Hispanic Antonio and the French Mexican Jean Baptiste Trudeau were also "foreigners" because they were born in an area that belonged to Mexico.

As was true of the majority of groups emigrating to the far West at this time, however, most of the Donner party were American-born inhabitants of the Mississippi Valley, the bulk of them from Illinois, Iowa, and Missouri. They, along with the foreign-born contingent of the party, constituted a quite representative cross section of pre–Civil War westering America.

By 1846, overland travelers had a fairly good notion of what to bring with them. The Donners and the other families and individuals who came to constitute their party started off with more than adequate provisions and belongings to see them through the journey and get them started in California. In addition to their wagons, draft animals (oxen, mules, and horses), and running gear, they brought a sufficient supply of food, clothing, agricultural implements, and household articles. Like most other emigrating parties, they took what was necessary, much that was practical but nonessential, and some items that were luxuries or of only sentimental value; James Reed's two-story "Pioneer Palace" was a veritable household on wheels. And also like many another emigrant group, particularly in the 1840s, they brought too much and had to abandon many of the possessions that were not absolutely necessary to survival along the way. Parties traveling later, especially after news of the Donners' disaster in the Sierra Nevada, tended to bring less—too often not enough.

Among the material goods carried by the Donner company, both necessary and not so necessary, were farm implements and seed; firearms (flintlock muskets, percussion-lock rifles, and pistols) and ammunition; tents; bedding; medicines; cooking utensils (stoves, kettles, Dutch oven); tableware (knives, forks, spoons, and porcelain-, glass-, and china-ware); axes and hatchets; nails and screws; tables, beds, and other furniture; sewing and darning supplies; looking glasses; rubber coats and hats; fishhooks; tobacco and pipes; a bale of calico; rugs; and jewelry. Patrick Breen and Jay Fosdick, the son-in-law of Franklin Graves, brought fiddles. Tamsen Donner packed books, watercolors, oil paints, and other supplies for the "young ladies seminary" she planned to establish in California. The Reeds took along "a good library of standard works." Some families brought their pet dogs. Reed was the only one to bring a blooded horse. The Donners carried knickknacks for trading with Indians and "rich stores of lace, muslins, silks, satins, velvets and like cherished fabrics" which they hoped to "exchange for Mexican land-grants." Tamsen Donner also noted that "linsey dresses are the most suitable for children. Indeed, if I had one, it would be acceptable."[13]

Although some of the Donner party families were beginning to run low on food before they reached the California mountains, the party as a whole had victuals sufficient for completing the journey under normal circumstances. The fare they consumed along the way was the same as that eaten by thousands of others journeying to California and Oregon.[14] Tamsen Donner wrote, "Bread has been the principal article of food in our camp. We laid in 150 lbs. of flour and 75 lbs. of meat for each individual." Although she worried that bread might run low, she reported that meat was abundant. "Rice and beans are good articles on the road—cornmeal, too, is very acceptable," she added. Coffee, tea, pepper, jerked beef, sugar, and crackers were other staples carried by party members. Even during the desperate time in the Sierra Nevada, Mrs. Reed was able to provide for her children a Christmas dinner of rice, dried apples, bacon, tripe, and white beans. Some of the families brought along cows, which provided milk and butter. En route the men supplemented the travelers' diet by shooting geese, ducks, buffalo, and other game. Charles T. Stanton caught a catfish on the Big Blue River.[15]

Before the gold rush, Independence, Missouri, was the favored outfitting and "jumping-off" place for overlanders. "I can give you no idea," wrote Tamsen Donner to her sister, "of the hurry of this place at this time. It is supposed there be 7000 waggons start from this place, this season." In addition to the supplies purchased there, each adult member of the Donner party received a Bible from the local chapter of the American Tract Society; the children were given New Testaments.[16]

Like the vast majority of overlanders, the Donner company began their journey in the spring, when the weather was most favorable and grass and water were most plentiful. They crossed the Missouri River at Independence, as did most of the families (the Breens, Murphys, Eddys, Kesebergs, and Wolfingers) and individuals who joined them along the way. The Graves family, who joined the Donner party in the Wasatch Mountains, crossed the Missouri at St. Joseph, which would become the principal departure point for emigrants in 1849 and 1850. In the 1850s Kanesville, Iowa (later called Council Bluffs), was the principal jumping-off point.[17]

After leaving Independence, the next major river to cross was the Kaw, or Kansas. Virginia Reed Murphy recalled that the ferry the company used was operated by Kaw Indians. More likely it was the one run by Charles Fish, a Shawnee.[18] In this early period of overland travel there were only a few regular ferries, but it wasn't long before several entrepreneurs, Indian and white, established and operated a number of them; still later, bridges replaced many of the ferries.

At Soldier Creek, on May 19, the nine wagons of the Donner party attached themselves to a caravan of emigrants led by William H. Russell. This large group also included Edwin Bryant, J. Quinn Thornton, former Missouri governor Lilburn W. Boggs, and others who became well-known names in the annals of western migration. Following the usual practice of emigrating companies, the members of the Russell train adopted a set of rules to govern themselves on the trail. They also established a "court of arbitration" to settle disputes and "try offenders against the peace and good order of the company."[19] The usual penalty for grave crimes was banishment—the punishment later meted out to James Reed for the slaying of John Snyder much further west.

The Russell party pushed on to the swollen Big Blue River, which they crossed with a makeshift craft they christened the "Blue River Rover."[20] Continuing northward along what was by then the customary route, they reached the Platte River, the main artery of western migration in the 1840–1860 era. As they traveled along the south bank (the Mormons and some later travelers used the north bank), the Donners and their fellow sojourners passed by the familiar landmarks of the trail: Courthouse Rock, Chimney Rock, Scott's Bluff, Independence Rock, Devil's Gate, and South Pass. They crossed the south and north forks of the Platte, and the Laramie and Sweetwater Rivers. At Forts Bernard, Laramie, and Bridger they stopped to rest, repair their wagons, and resupply. These were not forts in the military sense, but rather trading posts. Soon, however, the United States Army would erect and man a series of installations for the protection and convenience of the emigrants.

Over the many miles the party encountered other travelers, including Santa Fe traders, Indians, fur trappers, and returning overlanders. The latter, called "gobacks" or "turnarounds," were a common sight. Most had found the going too discouraging and had decided to turn back eastward.[21] The family of Edward Trimble, who had been traveling with the Graves family, turned back after he was killed by Pawnees.[22]

For the Donner party and the other companies within the Russell group, life on the trail brought the usual range of experiences for overlanders in the 1840s. The journey was marked by the customary mix of friendships and enmities, cooperation and selfishness, joys and hardships. Tamsen Donner reported that "we have of the best of people in our company, and some, too, that are not so good."[23] There were deaths, but no recorded births; among the former was Mrs. Reed's elderly and infirm mother, Sarah Keyes, who died near what would be Manhattan, Kansas. In the little leisure time they had, the emigrants read, observed the scenery, hunted, fished, drank, played the fiddle, and sang. Tamsen Donner wrote that although she was occasionally able to botanize and read, she cooked "a 'heap' more." Near Fort Laramie the emigrants celebrated the Fourth of July, then the nation's favorite holiday.[24]

Disputes were inevitable, and some led to the splintering off of several families and individuals. "At Indian Creek 20 miles from Independence," Charles T. Stanton observed, "these five companies [of the Russell group] all constituted one, but owing to desertions and quarrelling, they became broken into fragments; and now by accident we all again once more meet [on the Sweetwater] and grasp the cordial hand—old enmities are forgotten and good feeling prevails."[25]

Such splintering and regrouping was characteristic of overland travel in 1840–1860. Parties left groups and joined others with regularity. The leader of the so-called Russell group resigned as captain at the crossing of the South Platte and was replaced by former governor Boggs; Russell and others (including Hiram Miller, who had been traveling with the Donners) soon left the main body and pushed on separately for California. After it was believed that the danger from Indian attack had passed, parties felt freer to travel in smaller groups.

The Donners and their companions learned that communication with friends and relatives back home was quite possible even on the trail. Eastbound travelers commonly took emigrants' mail with them.[26] Eliza Donner Houghton remembered that trappers and traders "courteously offered to carry the company's mail to the nearest post-office." Tamsen Donner and Edwin Bryant took advantage of such offers and handed over letters to newspapers for which they were correspondents. The wife of J. Quinn Thornton gave a letter to a Shawnee Indian to take to the post office at Westport, Missouri, to be mailed from there to Quincy, Illinois. At Fort Laramie, Charles Stanton left a letter to his brother unfinished so that he might send it on with a party of returning Californians. Letters written at Independence Rock by Virginia Reed and Stanton were sent with Wales B. Bonney, who was returning east from Oregon.[27]

The Donner party observed another common form of trail communication as well: missives left on animal skulls, tree trunks, and sticks. The party found two such messages directed to them. The first, written by Lansford W. Hastings and stuck in a bush at Weber Canyon, advised them not to travel in the canyon, but rather to send a messenger to him so that he could return and guide them by an easier route through the mountains. (James Reed, Charles Stanton, and William Pike went ahead to find Hastings, who pointed out a possible path.) South of Salt Lake they noticed a board with a tattered paper pasted to it—a second communication from Hastings, informing them that it would take two days and two nights of hard riding to reach the next grass and water.[28]

With some exceptions (e.g., Edward Trimble, who was killed by Pawnees), overlanders usually found that their initial anxiety about Indians was unfounded. The experiences of the Donner party match those of most other emigrants. Virginia Reed Murphy remembered that "we suffered vastly more from fear of the Indians before starting than we did on the plains." Writing from "near the junction of the North and South Platte," Tamsen Donner told a friend, "We feel no fear of Indians. Our cattle graze quietly around our encampment unmolested. . . . The Indians frequently came to see us, and the chiefs of a tribe breakfasted at our tent this morning. All are so friendly that I cannot help feeling sympathy and friendship for them." Her husband, George, told a correspondent, "The Indians all speak friendly to us. Two braves breakfasted with us." Charles T. Stanton, writing from near Fort Laramie, told of gratifying a party of Sioux with gifts of tobacco. In later years, Eliza Donner Houghton recalled good relations with the Indians in this part of the journey; over one stretch Indians protected and escorted the party in exchange for cotton goods, tobacco, salt pork, and other items.[29]

Although the instances of conflict along the Oregon and California Trails have been greatly exaggerated, killings did occur. Between 1840 and 1860 an estimated 362 emigrants and 426 Indians were killed; in 1846, 4 whites and 20 Indians were slain.[30] Most of the hostile encounters between overlanders and Indians occurred west of South Pass, as the Donner party found out. They passed safely through the Shoshone country of eastern Nevada, and began to have problems with Indians only after they entered the lands of the Paiutes.[31] Along the Humboldt River Indians took, ran off, killed, or shot arrows into several of their cattle and horses. Even the "friendly" Indians who helped the Donner party put out a grass fire helped themselves to two oxen, one horse, and a shirt.

It is generally agreed that the problems that proved to be the undoing of the Donner party began when the group deviated from the established road to California, which itself was not very well established in 1846. In 1841 the Bartleson-Bidwell party left the Oregon Trail beyond Soda Springs, struck out over the desert north and west of the Great Salt Lake, and stumbled westward over the salt flats until they reached the Humboldt River. They followed this stream to its sink and, after abandoning their wagons and using pack animals, crossed through the Sierra Nevada either at Walker Pass or somewhere in the vicinity of Sonora Pass. Turning to the north, they arrived at the San Joaquin Valley in November.[32]

Luck was a major factor in the Bartleson-Bidwell party's successful journey. Although they demonstrated that it was possible for a wagon train to reach the mountains of California, they did little to help lay out a good route. In 1843 Joseph B. Chiles, a member of the Bartleson-Bidwell party, organized a California-bound wagon train and, with the help of mountain man Joseph Walker, laid out better pathways to the Pacific. From Fort Boise, Chiles took a group of horsemen up the Malheur River and thence down into the upper Sacramento Valley. The wagons, led by Walker, turned south from Fort Boise and reached and followed the Humboldt. After leaving their wagons, Walker's group crossed the Sierra Nevada with pack animals through the pass that now bears his name.[33]

Thus, it was obvious that the Humboldt was the most feasible path through the Great Basin, but it had yet to be demonstrated that wagons could make it across the Sierra. The Stevens-Townsend-Murphy party of 1844 laid out what essentially became the California Trail. Caleb Greenwood, an elderly mountain man, guided the eleven-wagon group and made two important improvements to the itinerary: a sixty-mile shortcut between South Pass and the Green River (the Greenwood cutoff), and the Raft River–Goose Creek route from Fort Hall to the Humboldt.

At the Humboldt Sink, Truckee, a Paiute headman, told Greenwood of a river that led to a pass through the mountains. The river (later named for Truckee) did indeed take them to a pass, which, although rough, could be negotiated by wagons. Most of the Stevens-Townsend-Murphy party crossed into California through that pass—now known as Donner Pass—and arrived at Sutter's Fort, although the deep snow forced some to leave their wagons in the mountains at Truckee (later Donner) Lake. Some of the party volunteered to spend the winter with the wagons and built a small log cabin for the purpose on a creek at the east end of the lake. They later lost heart, however, and crossed the mountains on foot. Illness forced one of the party, Moses Schallenberger, to return to the cabin, where he spent the winter alone, living on foxes, until he was rescued in the spring. In 1845 Greenwood hastened eastward and successfully guided a wagon train into California via the Truckee River route without having to desert any wagons.[34]

Even with the many delays and mishaps they experienced, the Donners and their fellow travelers probably would have reached their destination without undue adversity had they followed this proven path. Unfortunately, at Fort Bridger, the members chose to take the Hastings cutoff instead.

Cutoffs were no novelty in overland travel. From the earliest stages of Oregon–California migration onward, emigrants developed several real or supposed shortcuts to the Pacific. By 1860 there were numerous cutoffs and alternate routes branching out from the California and Oregon Trails; scarcely a year went by without a new one being created.[35] There were no fewer than twelve trails through the Sierra Nevada in 1860. Ironically, the Donner party itself hacked a trail through Emigrant Canyon that made passage through the Wasatch Mountains easier for later travelers.[36] Most such "improvements," however, were of little value in saving time or mileage. This was certainly true of the cutoff named for Lansford W. Hastings.

The popularity of Hastings's 1845 guidebook, *Emigrants' Guide to Oregon and California*, helps to explain why the majority of emigrants in 1846 chose California over Oregon.[37] Hastings's main object in writing the book was to publicize the glories of the Mexican province; certainly it played a major role in inducing the Donners, Reeds, and their companies to go there. According to the guidebook, travelers headed for California could save many miles if they turned southwest from Fort Bridger, swung south of the Great Salt Lake, crossed the Ruby Mountains, and traversed the desert until they reached the Humboldt River. Although Hastings himself had actually traversed this stretch of country (on horseback), his book did not necessarily advocate it as the best route; it was mentioned rather offhandedly—barely even a suggestion, really.

In any case, Hastings was out on the Overland Trail in 1846 and, as noted earlier, had sent messages to those trekking to California, offering to guide them over the cutoff. The Harlan-Young party, another contingent of the Russell group, took him up on the offer. The Donner party was moving too slowly to do so, but they determined nevertheless to shorten their journey by taking the relatively untested route without a guide. With much difficulty and after leaving behind many wagons, Hastings and the Harlan-Young party traveled over his cutoff, arrived at the Humboldt, and pushed on to California via the Truckee River route.[38]

For the Donner party, however, the Hastings cutoff was the scene of one disaster after another. Their luck scarcely improved after reaching the Humboldt, and misfortune dogged them for the remainder of their trek. The story of their abandonment of wagons, the killing of Snyder and other instances of friction, the death of Hardkoop, the loss of cattle, shortages of food and water, harassment by Indians, and a host of other calamities need not be repeated here. Yet it is well to point out that most of the misadventures experienced by the Donner party after Fort Bridger and before the ascent into the mountains are not particularly extraordinary when compared with those of most other overland emigrants. Those who stayed on the main trails to California and Oregon also found their way fraught with difficulties even under the most favorable circumstances, particularly the last arduous miles of the Humboldt River route and the infamous Forty-Mile Desert.

As for the Hastings cutoff, Gary Topping, a close student of the controversy surrounding it, has pointed out that emigrants continued to utilize the cutoff even after the Donner catastrophe, particularly in the first years of the gold rush. He concludes that it was "a usable route, but not a very desirable one." So evil was its reputation by 1850, however, that virtually all travelers shunned it after that year.[39]

3 : Archaeology of the Murphy Cabin

DONALD L. HARDESTY &
SUSAN LINDSTRÖM

The lake camp where the first two contingents of the Donner party spent the winter of 1846–1847 consisted of three log cabins scattered up to a half mile apart along the creek at the eastern end of Truckee (later Donner) Lake.[1] Two years earlier, the Stevens-Townsend-Murphy party had built a small cabin on the site, and Moses Schallenberger, a member of that party, spent the winter of 1844–1845 there. The Breen family took over the Schallenberger cabin, and the Kesebergs built a lean-to next to it. Two newly built cabins sheltered the rest of the group. The Murphy, Foster, Pike, and Eddy families lived in one (the Murphy cabin); the Graves and Reed families shared the other. In 1879, C. F. McGlashan and some survivors of the Donner party tragedy returned to the spot and dug into the sites of the Breen cabin and the Graves-Reed cabin. They left the Murphy cabin untouched because they were unable to dig through the marsh vegetation that covered the site. Recent archaeological studies, most of them conducted in 1984 by the University of Nevada, Reno, have produced images of the Murphy cabin. This chapter draws together the archaeological data gained through such studies and information from the documentary record to give a detailed picture of the Murphy cabin and its inhabitants.

Personal Reminiscences of the Murphy Cabin

Firsthand accounts give a few personal glimpses of the Murphy household. Mary Murphy, who was about thirteen years old at the time of the ordeal, recalled some of her life in the cabin years later in a letter to C. F. McGlashan: "Mother and I were left at the lake with five children [after three others left with the now-famous Forlorn Hope escape party]. We somehow managed to keep them alive, while in the other cabins people were dying every day. Christmas we had a meal of boiled bones and oxtail soup. After supper Mother was barely able to put the babies to bed, and later on that evening with brother William reading her favorite psalm from the Good Book, she became bedridden and seriously ill."[2] Mary's brother William gave a similar account of life in the cabin in his correspondence with McGlashan: "William G. Murphy describes how they gathered up the old, castaway bones of the cattle—bones from which all the flesh had been previously picked—and boiled, and boiled, and boiled them until they actually would crumble between the teeth, and were eaten. The little children, playing upon [the] fire-rug in his mother's cabin, used to cut off little pieces and then eat them. In this manner, before any one was fairly aware of the fact, the fire-rug was entirely consumed."[3]

Patrick Breen's diary, kept between November 20, 1846, and March 1, 1847, gives other personal glimpses of life at the lake camp.[4] The December 17 entry is the first that mentions the Murphy cabin: "Bill Murp[hy] returned from the mountain party last evening." (Murphy, along with several other members of the Murphy family, had left the day before, trying to walk over the mountains on improvised snowshoes with the Forlorn Hope party.) Breen's diary doesn't mention the cabin again until January 15: "Mrs. Murphy blind. Lanth[rom Murphy] not able to get wood has but one axe betwixt him & Keysburg, he moved to Murphys yesterday." The Murphy household continued to decline. Two days later Breen wrote: "Lanthrom crazy last night so bill says, Keysburg sent bill to get hides off his shanty & carry him home this morning."

The January 27 diary entry reads: "Keysburg sick & Lanthrom lying in bed the whole of his time dont have fire enough to Cook their hides. Bill & Sim. Murphy sick." On January 31 Breen recorded the death of Lanthrom Murphy "last night about 1 Oclock." Tragedy continued to stalk the Murphy household. The entries for February 5 and 6 note that "Eddys child died last night," and "Murphys folks or Keysburgs say they cant eat hides I wish we had enough of them Mrs. Eddy very weak." Mrs. Eddy died the next day. On February 9, Mrs. Murphy visited the Breen cabin: "Mrs. Murphy here this morning pikes child all but dead Milt at Murphys not able to get out of bed Keyburg never gets up says he is not able. John went down today to bury Mrs Eddy and child heard nothing from Graves for 2 or 3 days Mrs. Murphy just now going to

Graves." The February 10 entry says that "Milt Elliott died las[t] night at Murphys Shanty about 9 Oclock P.M. Mrs. Reid went there this morning to see after his effects." Breen wrote on February 14 that "John & Edwd. burried Milt. this morning in the snow," and on February 22 that "I burried pikes child this mor[n]ing in the snow it died 2 days ago."

The last two diary entries put an even grimmer complexion on the Murphys' household and living conditions. February 25: "Mrs. Murphy says the wolves are about to dig up the dead bodies at her shanty." February 26: "Mrs. Murphy said here yesterday that [she] thought she would commence on Milt. & eat him. I dont [think] that she has done so yet, it is distressing." The last entry in the diary is dated March 1, just before Breen and his family left the camp with a rescue party.

When William Eddy and William Foster arrived with the third relief party at the lake camp on March 13 or 14 (both had escaped earlier in the Forlorn Hope party), they found seven people alive in the Murphy cabin: Lewis Keseberg, Lavina Murphy,[5] Simon Murphy, Tamsen Donner, and the three little Donner girls, Georgia, Eliza, and Frances.[6] James Eddy and George Foster had died and had been cannibalized, leading William Eddy, perhaps unjustifiably, to accuse Keseberg of murdering his son. The following day, Simon Murphy and the three Donner children left with the third relief and Tamsen Donner returned to the Alder Creek camp to care for her dying husband, leaving only Lewis Keseberg and Lavina Murphy in the cabin.

Years later, Eliza P. Donner Houghton recalled the cabin's interior when she first moved there sometime in March 1847 (she was only three years old at the time): "How can one describe that fateful cabin, which was dark as night to us who had come in from the glare of day? We heard no welcome but were given a dreary resting place near the foot of the steps, just inside the open doorway, with a bed of branches to lie upon and a blanket to cover us. After we had been there a short time we could distinguish persons on other beds of branches and a man with bushy hair reclining beside a smoldering fire."[7] Presumably, the man with the bushy hair was Lewis Keseberg.

When William "Le Gros" Fallon arrived with the fourth relief party at the lake camp more than a month later, on April 17, Lavina Murphy was dead. The Murphy cabin had been abandoned, apparently sometime in late March or early April. Only Lewis Keseberg remained alive.[8] Keseberg, the last Donner party survivor to leave the mountain camps, left with the fourth relief on April 21.

What happened to the cabin after that is known only generally. General Stephen Watts Kearny's military detachment, traveling east from California, passed through the lake camp on June 22, 1847. The eyewitness observations of what the detachment saw and did there are attributed to Fallon, the leader of the fourth relief party, who was traveling with Kearny's group as a guide. In *What I Saw in California*, Edwin Bryant states that Fallon made the following comments to him: "A halt was ordered for the purpose of collecting and interring the remains. Near the principal cabins I saw two bodies entire, with the exception that the abdomens had been cut open and the entrails extracted. . . . Strewn around the cabins were dislocated and broken skulls. . . . The remains were collected . . . and buried. . . . They were interred in a pit which had been dug in the center of one of the cabins for a cache. . . . the cabins were fired."[9] That all of this took place seems certain since other members of the detachment also documented the event.[10] Sergeant Nathaniel Jones, for example, recorded in his journal on June 22, 1847, that

> we came down the lake to some cabins that had been built by some emigrants last fall. They were overtaken in the snow. There were 80 of them in number and only 30 of them that lived. The rest of them starved to death. The general called a halt and ordered 5 men to bury the deserted bodies that were lying on the ground. Those who lived the longest lived on the dead bodies of the others. One man lived about four months on human flesh. This place now goes by the name of cannibal camp. . . . Col. Fremont passed us here, the first time we have seen him since we reached Fort Sutter. After we had buried the bones of the dead we set fire to the cabin. I started about two in the afternoon came 7 miles and camped. One mile above here there was another cabin and more dead bodies, but the general did not order them buried.[11]

Historians of the Donner party believe that it was the Murphy cabin that was burned. C. F. McGlashan's *History of the Donner Party*, for example, states that "the big rock against which the Murphy cabin stood is half hidden by willows and by fallen tamaracks, whose branches are interlaced so as to form a perfect net-work above the place where the cabin stood. Under the floor of this cabin the remains of the poor victims are supposed to have been buried."[12] Nevertheless, records left by emigrants who passed the remains of the camp at Donner Lake during the next couple of years are unclear about which of the cabins was burned or even whether the burial actually took place. Henry William Bigler, for example, a member of the Mormon Battalion who traveled through the campsite on September 5, 1847, just a few months after the alleged burial, made the following entry in his diary:

> Passing down the mountain to the head of Truckee River some six or eight miles, we came to a shanty built last winter, and about this cabin we found the skeletons of several human beings. I discovered a hand. It was nearly entire. It had been partly burned to a crisp. The little finger was not burnt.

The flesh seemed to be a little dried. I judged it to be the hand of a woman. I do not believe that the wolves disturbed them. The place had the appearance that they had been burned after death.[13]

Bigler's observations suggest that the cabin, which could have been the Murphy cabin, was burned but that human remains had not been buried in it. The implication is that General Kearny's party simply piled the remains in the cabin and burned them—that there was no burial in a mass grave. Other emigrant diaries suggest that it was not the Murphy cabin that was burned. Emigrant John Markle, for example, who was traveling west on the California Trail, recorded the following in his diary on August 20, 1849:

> Today we travelled about 10 miles and camped in a valley at the base of the mountain about ¾ mile east of Truckee Lake. The first 2 miles brought us to the valley where Donner camped. One mile more brought us opposite to where his cabins were, which were situated about 1 or 2 miles from the road on the righthand side. There were any number of fragments left but more human bones than anything. Six miles more and we came to where the Graves family wintered and all perished except 5 and 2 of them died after they got through. The road now leaves and we came to Fosters and Breen's cabins where they camped. The road now leaves them to the right, but the old road runs just past, leaving them on the left.
>
> Graves and Fosters cabins are the only ones that are standing yet and they represent a gloomy appearance. In Foster's cabin there were old cloth[e]s which were worn by females and, also, long female hair which appeared as if it had fallen from the head, and any quantity of bones in and around the cabin.[14]

The Markle diary strongly suggests that the Breen cabin, which was not standing when he passed by, was the one burned by the Kearny expedition. Of course, how Markle knew who lived in each of the two remaining cabins is an issue.

Other travelers who passed through the lake camp at about the same time observed that the Graves-Reed cabin was standing, along with one of the two cabins closest to Donner Lake; unfortunately, they usually did not specify which one.[15] One exception is Augustus Ripley Burbank, who appears to have been the only emigrant diarist to record a visit to the Murphy cabin site and who made the following observation on September 10, 1849:

> The donor [sic] cabins stood 200 yards above the road & some distance from the Lake. Their remains or ashes & the bottom logs are only to be seen to designate to the passing traveler the spot where the painful sufferings occured (Mr. Fremont, it is said, burnt the cabin). ¼ of a mile below near the stream or outlet, & on the East side of a large oveling [sic] rock is

an other cabin (it is a standing) the bones & hornes of oxen lay thick about the door. These cabins in this vicinity have been covered with logs, brush & C. The stumps of fallen trees near the fronts of the cabins, stand at the height of 5 & 10 feet, Some probably over the latter, showing the depth of the snow when the trees was fallen for fire wood. (The history of these melancholy looking cabins & places are two well known).[16]

Without question, it is the Murphy cabin ("on the East side of a large oveling rock") that Burbank's diary describes as still standing in 1849. Burbank's journal entry also implies that the Breen cabin contains the mass grave. Support for that interpretation comes from the 1984 UNR excavation of the Murphy cabin site, discussed later in this chapter, which uncovered no evidence of a grave.

The Murphy cabin burned sometime between 1847 and 1872, the year when the *Truckee Republican* reported that "all the [Donner] cabins have been burned down or carried away by relic collectors."[17] C. F. McGlashan located the cabin remains in 1879 after interviews and a visit to the site with some of the survivors. He did not excavate the site, however, because the dense swamp grass resisted his spade, and the spot appears to have remained untouched until 1893.[18] McGlashan relates what happened then: "On the 12th day of August, 1893, . . . I took up the last remaining log of the Murphy cabin and conveyed it to my residence. Six logs of this cabin were in place in 1879, but all had decayed and vanished except the log on the western side of the cabin, the one containing the threshold of the door. With the assistance of the ladies of Truckee, five thousand small vials were filled with the partially decayed wood of this log, and these, together with the remnant of the log, were placed in the Rocking Stone Tower."[19] Some of the remaining vials now reside in the Pioneer Museum at Donner Memorial State Park.

Traveling the Archaeological Road

In 1984 the University of Nevada, Reno, in cooperation with the state of California Department of Parks and Recreation and with the sponsorship of the National Geographic Society, began an archaeological study at the spot marked by McGlashan as the site of the Murphy cabin, which is now preserved as part of Donner Memorial State Park (Figure 4).[20] Students taking a class in archaeological field methods did the work, together with volunteers from the local community, the Truckee-Donner Historical Society, and state and federal agencies (Figure 5). The study started with an inventory of the artifacts and other physical remains that covered the ground surface at the cabin site. Virtually nothing other than quite recent twentieth-century artifacts was found. Next, the archaeologists probed what lay beneath the surface by removing, at regular intervals, several small soil samples, which were analyzed to determine

Figure 4: The rock at the Murphy cabin site. The rock, which is ten and a half feet high, formed the western wall of the cabin. Photograph ©1997 Peter Goin.

Figure 5: The Murphy cabin site excavation in progress, 1984. The rock that formed the western wall of the cabin is on the left.

their chemical composition. The samples with high levels of exchangeable and total phosphates, acid-soluble calcium, and organic matter, suggesting decomposed bone and wood, pointed out the most likely whereabouts of the cabin. After establishing a site datum, or permanent reference point, the field team then laid out a checkerboard-like grid over the surface of the cabin site. The grid of one-meter squares provided the framework on which to map the exact location of artifacts and other objects found during the excavation. Excavators then used trowels and other small tools to slowly dig away the soil matrix. They dug each of the one-meter grid squares stratigraphically—that is, by discrete soil layers or units representing depositional events, when these were visible or otherwise identifiable. In the absence of such layers, the excavators dug in five-centimeter increments. Artifacts and other objects were mapped in place whenever possible. The excavators then sifted the soil through a fine-mesh (⅛-inch) screen and removed artifacts, bone fragments, and other objects of human origin for later laboratory analysis. They also placed samples of the excavated deposits in a water flotation tank to recover plant remains and other very small and light materials.

Archaeological Images of the Murphy Cabin

The key to interpreting the physical remains of the Murphy cabin is their archaeological context—the material matrix containing the remains along with their location and associations. Artifacts and other physical remains may be found in either a primary context or a secondary context.[21] The primary, or undisturbed, context of artifacts and other archaeological remains from the Murphy cabin site includes the acquisition, manufacture, use, disposal, and deposition of artifacts by the people who lived in the cabin. In contrast, the secondary context includes natural and human disturbances that occurred after the cabin was abandoned, such as the salvage activities of the fourth relief party, the burning of the cabin, relic collecting and other visitor activities, and the removal of the bottom logs in 1893. Ten distinctive layers of refuse, ash and charcoal, soils, and other materials, along with unidentified pits, a fire pit, postholes, and artifact clusters, define the archaeological context of the Murphy cabin remains (Figures 6 and 7).

POSTABANDONMENT DEPOSITS

The natural and cultural processes that took place after the Murphy cabin was abandoned in 1847 formed five layers that were revealed by the excavation. Of these, the topmost layer, stratum 1, is a thin layer of duff originating in the forest litter fall that covers the existing ground surface. Below the duff layer are another four layers covering most of the northern and southern ends of the cabin site. Two of the layers, strata 2 and 3, contain twentieth-century artifacts

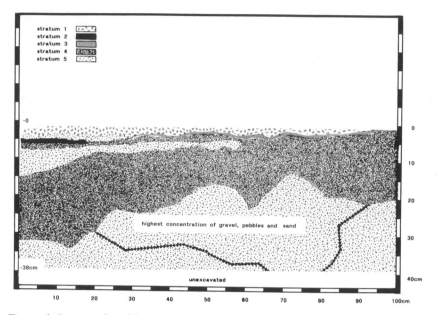

Figure 6: Stratigraphy of the Murphy cabin site. Stratum 1 is forest duff; strata 2 and 3 are twentieth-century deposits of red cinders and decomposed granite; stratum 4 is a dark organic layer deposit marking the cabin's earthen floor that contains artifacts and bone dating to the Donner party period; and stratum 5 is a silty loam predating the Donner party occupation.

that probably reflect past efforts by Donner Memorial State Park staff to consolidate the marshy ground to enable visitors to walk more easily over the site; however, we were unable to find records verifying that. Stratum 2 is white decomposed granite lying just below the forest duff at the south end of the cabin site. Stratum 3 is a stratigraphically correlated layer of red cinders at the north end of the site, extending northward along the present pathway to the park's Pioneer Museum. Strata 2 and 3 vary in thickness from a thin veneer in the middle of the site to as much as ten centimeters toward the edges.

The next two layers revealed by the excavation also formed after the cabin was abandoned in 1847. Just below the white decomposed granite and east of the southwest corner of the rock wall is a layer of thick yellow clay (feature 8). The clay layer, which extends over an area of about six square meters, covers part of a shallow pit designated during the 1984 excavation as feature 9. Feature 9 is visible in a 1918 photograph of the bronze plaque on the rock wall, so the clay deposit must have been added after 1918. At the base of the northwest corner of the rock wall is a rockfall layer (feature 7) that lies directly over the artifacts from the Donner party's occupation of the cabin. Historical photographs taken at different times show that the rockfall is the result of defoliation of the rock wall of the Murphy cabin. Several large fragments of cut bone were located under the rockfall, suggesting that it has provided some protection from relic collectors.

COLLAPSED LOG WALL DEPOSITS

Charred wood, charcoal, and ash deposits from the burning of the cabin sometime between 1847 and 1872 formed three of the features uncovered during the excavation. The largest (feature 12) is a charred log fragment about two meters long and one-half meter wide that lies directly on the cabin floor (stratum 4); it may have been the remnants of a log from the east wall of the cabin or a roof support beam. Two thick charcoal-ash deposits were located as well. Feature 13 lies just below the white decomposed granite (stratum 2) and on top of the cabin floor (stratum 4) at the north end of the site. The charcoal-ash layer is very thin on the inside, southern edge, and thickens to about twenty centimeters outward toward the north and outside the cabin floor. Feature 14 lies just below the red cinders (stratum 3) at the south end of the site and on top of stratum 4. Like feature 13, the charcoal-ash layer is very thin on the inside, northern, edge and thickens to about fifteen centimeters outward toward the south and outside the cabin floor.

What do the deposits suggest about the architecture of the Murphy cabin? Fire investigators who have studied recent log cabin fires have provided guidelines that can account for the distribution of ash, charcoal, charred wood, and the uncharred but decayed wood observed in the archaeological record.[22] Generally, log structures do not burn like wooden frame buildings, whose walls tend to collapse inward or outward en masse; log walls, being supported by their corner notches, tend instead to fall down in place. The fire burns hottest highest up in the structure, and the upper logs may be incinerated to ash. The fire cools as it approaches the ground, leaving larger pieces of charcoal and segments of charred wood in place. Green logs make an even cooler fire. The logs closest to the bottom have the best chance of surviving a cabin fire, and the notched corners, which represent the densest concentration of wood, have a greater tendency to be preserved in place. Sill logs may even survive uncharred, as was the case with the Murphy cabin.[23] Application of these principles of log cabin burning to the archaeological remains of the Murphy cabin suggests that the areas of thickest charcoal deposits and greatest concentration of charred wood fragments mark the walls of the cabin. Variables such as the type and amount of fuel, how and when the fire was set, and the amount of external wind and internal ventilation, however, could affect these expectations.

THE CABIN FLOOR LAYER

Another physical image of the architecture of the Murphy cabin is a thin, dark organic layer (stratum 4) marking the dirt floor which contains most of the

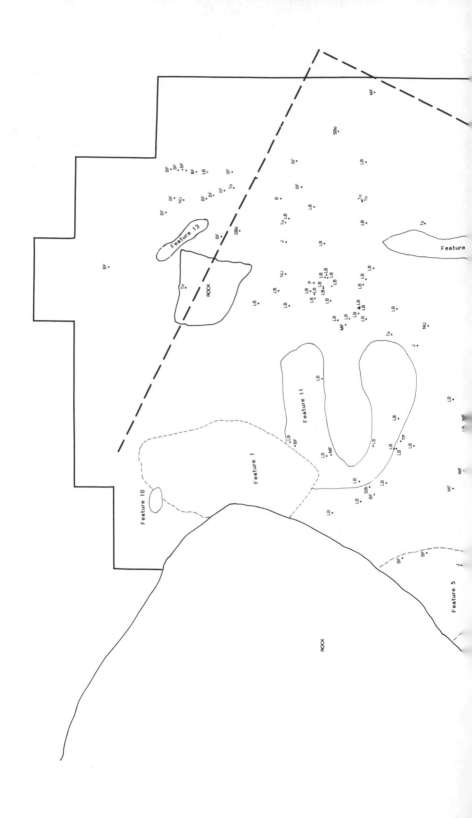

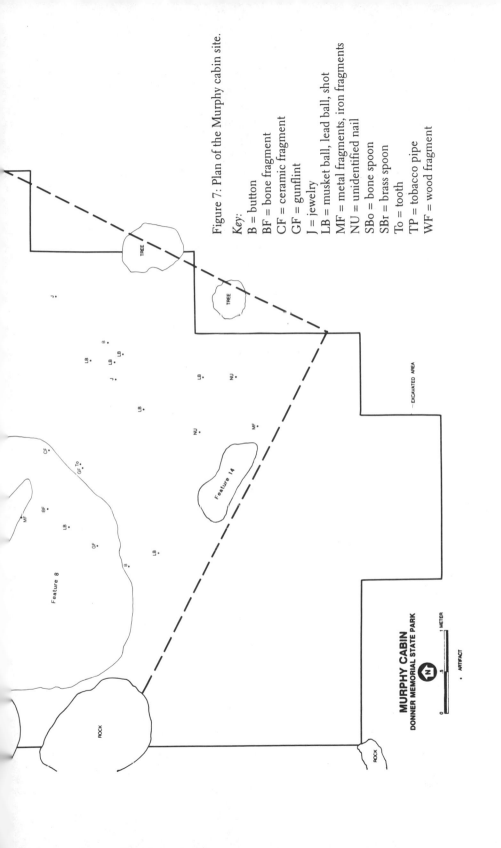

Figure 7: Plan of the Murphy cabin site.

Key:
B = button
BF = bone fragment
CF = ceramic fragment
GF = gunflint
J = jewelry
LB = musket ball, lead ball, shot
MF = metal fragments, iron fragments
NU = unidentified nail
SBo = bone spoon
SBr = brass spoon
To = tooth
TP = tobacco pipe
WF = wood fragment

MURPHY CABIN
DONNER MEMORIAL STATE PARK

ARTIFACT

artifacts and other archaeological remains. The floor layer, which varies in thickness from one to five centimeters, lies below the white decomposed granite and red cinders (strata 2 and 3) at the north and south ends of the cabin and the forest litter (stratum 1) in the middle. The boundaries of this floor deposit—along with the distribution of artifacts, charred wood, and ash—can be used to estimate the boundaries of the Murphy cabin floor. Figure 7 shows the distribution of Donner party artifacts found in the cabin floor layer.

PRE–DONNER PARTY ALLUVIAL LAYER

Below the cabin floor is a layer of mottled, yellowish brown silty loam with some clay lenses (stratum 5) that contains no Donner party remains. It appears to be the water-laid deposits of Donner Creek. Several basalt flakes and a basalt biface from earlier Native American occupations were found up to a meter below the cabin floor.

PITS

Two pits found in stratum 4 both appear to have been formed long after the Donner party left the camp. Feature 9 is a V-shaped pit that is oriented perpendicular to the rock wall of the cabin and is filled with a loose, dark gray, loamy soil containing a few bone fragments, modern bottle glass fragments, wood fragments, and metal foil. Several large rocks covered the top of the pit. The pit cuts into the fire pit (feature 5) at the base of the rock wall, and the yellow clay layer (feature 8) lies directly on top of part of the pit. Without question the pit was dug after the Donner party occupied the cabin. Most likely, it dates to the twentieth century. A 1918 photograph shows visitors standing in the open pit and looking at the bronze plaque on the big rock.[24]

Feature 10 is a small, circular pit at the extreme northwest end of the cabin. The inside of the pit, which is only about one-half meter in diameter, yielded only modern artifacts and fill, including red cinders, a well-preserved wooden stake with a sharpened end, and colorless glass bottle fragments. Without question, the pit is of recent origin and contains no information about the Murphy cabin.

FIRE PITS

The excavators found another pit (feature 5)—shallow, bowl-shaped and filled with ash, charcoal, and calcined bone fragments—next to the southwestern corner of the big rock. This semicircular pit appears to be associated with the Donner party period. It is approximately one meter in diameter and one-half meter deep and has been cut by the feature 9 pit. Most likely feature 5 is a fire pit; certainly the big rock against which the cabin was built provided a ready-made chimney and hearth. Excavators found a line of heavy concentrations of charcoal, ash, and crushed calcined bone extending along the base of the big rock on both sides of feature 5 that suggests a "hearth row" rather than a single fire pit. More than one fire may have been burning at the same time within the cabin, and water seepage down the slanted face of the rock wall may have forced the relocation of the fire pit from time to time.

POSTHOLES

Two postholes were found at the bases of the northeast and southeast corners of the rock wall. These appear to be the sites of vertical "cribbing" poles used to support the floating ends of the log walls running from the rock outward to the corner of the intersecting walls of the cabin.

ARTIFACT CLUSTERS

Spatial clusters of artifacts define another archaeological context. Excavators found three artifact clusters at the Murphy cabin. The largest cluster was more or less in front of the rock wall and the hearth row. Two smaller clusters were found in the vicinity of the northeast corner of the cabin floor, one close to the center of the north wall and the other in the east wall near the corner. Personal artifacts such as clothing, tobacco pipes, and items of adornment dominate all three clusters. The artifacts found in and around the decayed "ghost" of a large tree root system (feature 11), however, consist mostly of firearms equipment, especially lead balls. Nineteenth-century photographs of the rock show the jagged stump of a tree, which may have been incorporated into the cabin, still in place. Perhaps the cabin's occupants placed an ammunition pouch in this part of the cabin, and the pouch gradually disintegrated and released its contents to slowly migrate downward into the soft earth of the decaying root system. Or perhaps the cluster of artifacts merely reflects the vagaries of preservation; more or less randomly distributed artifacts within the cabin may have become "invisible" to visitors intent on collecting relics—and were thus preserved—as they moved down into the root system. If that were the case, however, the cluster should include relatively large numbers of other kinds of artifacts as well, and it does not.[25]

Artifact Images of the Murphy Cabin

The Murphy cabin excavators found a disproportionately large number of lead balls and other firearms-related artifacts. Written accounts of the Donner party state that its members carried six-shooters, a pepper box pistol, a rifle gun, a muzzle loader, caps, bullets, and a powder horn.[26] When McGlashan and several survivors of the tragedy dug into the Graves-Reed cabin in 1879, they found several firearms-related artifacts: "A brass pistol, single barreled, apparently a century old, was found under the Graves cabin, and near it an old flintlock. In the corner of the fire-place of the Reed cabin were found several bul-

Figure 8: Catholic religious medal from the Murphy cabin site.

lets and number two shot. Gun-flints, ready for use or in a crude form, were found in each of the cabins."[27] Emigrant parties traveling overland in the 1840s often carried Hawken and Henry rifles; both large-caliber plains weapons were popular during that period.[28] That the Donner party did as well is suggested by a Hawken rifle, presently in the possession of the California Department of Parks and Recreation, that is said to have belonged to a member of the group. In addition, the many round lead balls in the .50- to .60-caliber range found by excavators suggest that large-caliber firearms were present. Most of these balls, however, are somewhat larger than the usual Hawken size of .50 to .53 caliber.[29] The excavators also found gunflints but no percussion caps at the Murphy cabin. Chapter 5 has a detailed discussion of the firearms fragments found at the cabin site.

Tobacco pipe fragments are the next most common category of artifacts with identifiable uses found at the cabin. Written accounts of the Donner party mention tobacco smoking several times. Perhaps the best known describes Charles Stanton sitting by the campfire and smoking his pipe just before he died from starvation and exposure.[30] Most of the tobacco pipe fragments found at the Murphy cabin are long-stemmed white kaolin clay "Dublin" pipes, the most common type in the nineteenth century. Four of them are marked with "T," "TD," or "D" impressed into the bowl or stem. Such marks, usually attributed either to Thomas Dennis of Bristol, England, or to Thomas Dormer of London, first appeared in the early eighteenth century.[31] The only other pipe found by the excavators is a gray ceramic bowl with two grooves and rows of repeated circles; the bowl was used with a detachable reed stem.

Beads, jewelry, toiletries, and other personal artifacts constitute another common artifact category found at the Murphy cabin. The thirteen colored glass and ceramic beads in the collection probably came from necklaces. Other ornamental artifacts include a silver-plated dangling earring or pendant, a brooch, and a vulcanite hairpin. Toiletries include comb fragments and what appears to be bone tweezers; pocket knife fragments were also found in the cabin remains. Perhaps the most unique artifact found by the Murphy cabin excavators is a Roman Catholic religious medal (Figure 8). Richard Ahlborn of the National Museum of American History at the Smithsonian Institution examined the medal and found it to be stylistically similar to those made in the United States between 1825 and 1875 and used by Roman Catholics. Such medals were stamped out from a base metal and then plated with tin or silver. Ahlborn also reported that

> the representation of Jesus, encircled by the inscription "SWEET HEART OF JESUS HAVE MERCY ON US" and of His Mother, encircled by "BLESSED VIRGIN MARY PRAY FOR US" are typical in both gesture and sentiment of the mid-nineteenth century. These representations somewhat anticipate the popular sacred-heart themes, as they did not become official Catholic dogma until about 1875. . . . Finally, the suspension loop lies in the same plane as the medal, unlike earlier medals with cross-set hangers. The loose wire loop is also typical of the 19th century in its size and structure.[32]

Whether the medal belonged to someone in the Donner party is unknown. Written accounts describe Mrs. Lavina Murphy as a Baptist who had converted to Mormonism in Tennessee and make no mention of any member of the Murphy, Eddy, Foster, or Pike families being Catholic.[33] The Breen family, who lived next door and certainly visited the Murphy cabin, was the only Catholic family in the Donner party, although Virginia Reed Murphy, who stayed with the Breens at one point during the winter entrapment, later converted to Catholicism.[34]

The cabin remains contain several items related to clothing. Of these, buttons are by far the most common. The other artifacts in this category include a heel from a small shoe, four shoe grommets, a cloth buttonhole, and two coat studs. Nails, screws, tacks, rivets, staples, and washers, probably used as fasteners in the construction of household furnishings such as chests or trunks, cabinets, and the like, form another common artifact category found at the Murphy cabin. Cut nails dominate this category. An iron key, possibly from a chest or trunk, was also found in the cabin remains.

Fragments of glass food and medicine bottles form the other major category of artifacts found at the Murphy cabin. The artifacts include cobalt blue octagonal bottles, colorless vials, and cathedral pickle bottles. Surprisingly few artifacts of items used for food storage, preparation, and consumption were

Table 2: Vertebrate Remains from the Murphy Cabin Site

Context	Taxon	Element	NISP[1]
Stratum 1	*Bos taurus*	Teeth	10
		Podials	2
		Total fragments	12
Strata 1–3	*Bos taurus*	Teeth	17
Feature 8	*Bos taurus*	Mandible	2
		Scapula	1
		Tarsals	1
		Tibia	1
		Teeth	1
		Total fragments	6
	Ursus sp.	Phalanges	2
Stratum 4	*Bos taurus*	Carpals	1
		Femur	2
		Innominate	1
		Mandible	3
		Metacarpals	2
		Metapodials	1
		Metatarsals	1
		Phalanges	2
		Rib	2
		Sesamoid	2
		Tarsals	6
		Tibia	4
		Teeth	56
		Total fragments	83
	Equus sp.	Teeth	1
	Ursus sp.	Caudal vertebrae	2
		Metapodials	1
		Metatarsals	1
		Phalanges	8
		Sesamoid	1
		Teeth	1
		Total fragments	14
Strata 4–5	*Bos taurus*	Radius	1
Stratum 5	*Bos taurus*	Teeth	1
Mixed	*Bos taurus*	Teeth	4
Total fragments in all layers			141

1. NISP = number of identified specimens.

found, however. Ceramic tableware from the site includes what is probably a fragment from a dinner plate decorated with a red transfer-printed floral design, a handle from an undecorated whiteware cup, and an unidentified whiteware fragment. The cabin deposits also included table utensils in the form of brass spoon fragments, a strap handle from a green salt-glazed stoneware jug—probably a food container rather than tableware—and a fragment of a cast iron cooking pot. In contrast, McGlashan found a wide variety of ceramic tableware at the Breen cabin, most of it decorated with the painted sprig designs popular in the 1840s, and other domestic artifacts such as spoons, knives, forks, a darning needle, straight pins, a sewing awl, and glass tumblers.[35]

Animal Remains

Some of the most intriguing material images of the Murphy cabin household come from the animal bone fragments recovered during the excavation. Amy Dansie of the Nevada State Museum first analyzed the animal remains from the Murphy cabin site in 1984.[36] More recently, Donald K. Grayson of the University of Washington reanalyzed the remains and reached essentially the same conclusions (see Appendix 1). Both analyses indicate that the identifiable bone and teeth from the cabin site are from three species: cattle (*Bos taurus*), horse or mule (*Equus* sp.), and bear (*Ursus* sp.) (see Table 2). Cattle bones were by far the most common animal remains, followed by foot and tail bones from bear. Written records indicate that at least two bears were killed by the Donner party in the mountain camps, one at the lake camp and the other at the Alder Creek camp. William Eddy, who occupied the Murphy cabin, killed a bear in mid-November 1846. The bear bones at the Murphy cabin site may have come from two individuals, perhaps including the one killed at Alder Creek. Finally, there was one tooth from a horse or mule in the animal remains.

The condition of the animal bones suggests several things about how the animals were used by the Donner party at the mountain camps. Many of the cattle bones had been fractured into large pieces, suggesting the extraction of marrow without further use of the bones. The Murphy cabin excavators also found evidence that some of the bones, found in the hearths and charred white, had been used as fuel. In addition, there is both documentary and archaeological evidence that bones were boiled or charred for food. As noted previously, for example, in letters to C. F. McGlashan, survivors Mary Murphy and William Murphy recalled eating "boiled bones" during their ordeal in the mountain camps. The Murphy cabin excavators also found evidence of that practice. There is no evidence, however, that the bones were ground into meal, a traditional winter famine food among the Washoe and other Great Basin Indians.[37] The animal remains recovered from the Dangberg site, a historic Washoe winter village, for example, consist mostly of the very small fragments produced by grinding or crushing in manos and metates.[38] Only large bone fragments were found at the Murphy cabin site.

Human Remains

What about human remains? Dr. Sheilagh Brooks, a forensic anthropologist from the University of Nevada, Las Vegas, examined the bone fragments for morphological evidence that they are human remains, but the fragments are so small and so deteriorated that she was unable to determine their origin. Still, Dr. Brooks suspected that some of the fragments are human bone, and she turned to biochemical methods to settle the question. Dr. Jerold Lowenstein of the University of California School of Medicine in San Francisco analyzed several of these fragments using radioimmunoassay, a technique that uses identifiable collagen, albumin, transferrin, and fibronectin to classify small bone fragments to species.[39] Of the four fragments considered to be most humanlike, two turned out to be human; the other two are bovine.[40] Dr. Lowenstein later examined several other questionable bone fragments from the cabin site. Of the three he was able to identify to species, one is human.[41]

Nothing immortalizes the Donner party more than the alleged practice of cannibalism of the dead at the mountain camps and during the survivors' escape attempts. The Murphy cabin is one of the places where it supposedly occurred. Patrick Breen, for example, recorded in his diary on February 26, 1847, that "Mrs. Murphy said here yesterday that [she] thought she would commence on Milt [Elliott, one of the dead teamsters] & eat him." The rescue party led by James Reed seemed to confirm that she had done just that when it found Elliott's mutilated body at the door of the cabin three days later. Certainly it is possible to detect cannibalism archaeologically through, for example, the occurrence of minute cut marks on bone. Unfortunately, the Murphy cabin bone fragments are so fragmented and so deteriorated that they offer no information on the matter.

The results of the Murphy cabin excavation do shed light on one other question about human remains, however. As discussed earlier in this chapter, written accounts describe the men of General Kearny's detachment burying the remains of the Donner party dead that lay scattered around one of the cabins at the lake camp. The remains were said to have been buried inside one of the cabins, which was then burned. The excavators of the Murphy cabin site, however, found no evidence of a mass grave. That fact, together with the evidence contained in the diaries of John Markle and Augustus Burbank, which imply that only the Graves-Reed and Murphy cabins still stood in 1849, suggests that the grave actually is at the Breen cabin. The grave may have been destroyed during early excavations or during the erection of Pioneer Monument in 1909, or it may still be there.

Murphy Cabin Architecture

Written, pictorial, cartographic, and other documentary accounts give some clues to the architecture and physical appearance of the Murphy cabin. Of these, the most detailed is the 1880 sketch of the lake camp published in Thompson and West's *History of Nevada County, California*. The image apparently came from the recollections of William Murphy, who was eleven years old when he lived in the cabin.[42] Murphy's sketch shows the cabin as a rectangular building built against a pyramid-shaped rock and aligned more or less parallel with Donner Creek; the sketch also shows the Murphy cabin as the smallest of the three cabins at the lake camp. The cabin in the drawing has a flat roof that appears to be covered with animal skins, canvas, and tree branches; it has a door opening at the end of the cabin that faces away from the lake, but no windows. How the cabin was arranged inside is less clear from documentary sources. William Murphy, for example, remembered it as a "one room shanty";[43] Virginia Reed Murphy, who never lived there, recalled that "all of the cabins were double."[44] Perhaps the most detailed account of the inside of the cabin was given by Eliza P. Donner Houghton, who was only three years old when she lived for a short time at the cabin sometime in March 1847. She remembered "a bed of branches to lie upon" just inside the open doorway and "a man with bushy hair reclining beside a smouldering fire."[45] Whether the branches were placed on crude beds or cots is unknown; however, cots apparently were used at the Breen cabin. In 1849, for example, a visitor to the cabin observed that "two or three cot bedsteads made of poles were still standing in the cabin."[46]

Written accounts that describe how the other two cabins at the lake camp were built provide indirect evidence of the Murphy cabin's construction. The Graves-Reed cabin, for example, appears to have been double, with two rooms sharing a common interior wall. William C. Graves recalled that "father's cabin was built double, a fireplace at each end," and that each of the rooms was "about 16 feet square."[47] Several forty-niners who passed by the cabin gave similar descriptions. On August 22, 1849, for example, Vincent Geiger and Wakeman Bryarly recorded in their diary that the cabin "was two in one, there being a separation of logs in between."[48] Also in 1849, Joseph Wood observed the "walls of a double log cabin";[49] and Charles Parke noted that "the house is built of logs and divided into apartments."[50] Bryarly and Geiger's diary further describes the cabin as follows: "The timbers were from 8 inches to a foot in diameter, about 8 or 9 ft. high & covered over with logs upon which had been placed branches & limbs of trees, dirt, etc. The logs were fitted very nicely together, there being scarcely a crevice between."[51]

The Breen cabin was rectangular. At one end was a single room and a chimney, at the other a lean-to shed constructed by Lewis Keseberg. The main cabin, built earlier by the Stevens-Townsend-Murphy party, was nearly square and had one door, suggesting a slightly elongated version of the traditional Finnish floor plan.[52] Moses Schallenberger, a member of the Stevens-Townsend-Murphy party who spent the winter of 1844–1845 in the cabin, recalled that "Foster, Montgomery, and Schallenberger built the cabin. Two days were spent in its construction. It was built of pine saplings, and roofed with pine

Figure 9: Artist's reconstruction of the Murphy cabin. Illustration ©1997 John Betz. Reconstruction based on a rough sketch by Craig Meacham. The illustration does not show doorway detail since archaeological evidence provided no information about how the "floating" ends of logs in the doorway were supported.

brush and rawhides. It was twelve by fourteen feet, and seven or eight feet high, with a chimney in one end, built 'western style.' One opening, through which light, air, and the occupants passed, served as both window and door."[53]

Comparative studies of folk architecture provide another source of information about the Murphy cabin. The construction of the log cabins at the lake camp depended to some extent on folk architecture traditions common at the time. Most members of the Donner party were from woodland regions of the United States that were most strongly influenced by English and Scotch-Irish log cabin–building traditions.[54] In the English tradition, the basic one-room, or single-pen, cabin was "distinguished by side-facing gables, front and rear doors centered in each eave wall, and square shape, with each wall between 15 and 16 feet in length."[55] Either a chimney was attached to one gable end, or a smoke hole was left in the roof. The Scotch-Irish tradition was similar, but the cabin plan was rectangular "with eave walls five or six feet longer than the gabled sides. The doors of the Scotch-Irish cabin were positioned off-center, producing asymmetry that was absent from the English plan."[56] Cabin size varied, but typical Scotch-Irish cabins were about twelve by twenty feet. Both plans could have been known to almost any of the Donner party. Two-room, or double-pen, log cabins also would have been part of the folk architecture traditions known to the Donner party. The square English plan—but not the rectangular Scotch-Irish plan—was easily enlarged into a double-pen cabin. Typically, one of three variants of the English floor plan was followed in building a two-room cabin: (1) the "Cumberland" house, with two rooms sharing a common wall with chimneys at both ends; (2) the saddle-bag house, with two rooms sharing a chimney in the middle; or (3) the dog-trot house, with an open hallway or passage between two rooms. All three cabin types were widespread throughout woodland America at the time and could have been known to almost any of the Donner party.[57]

By combining the documentary and archaeological evidence, artist John Betz was able to construct a reasonably detailed image of the Murphy cabin (Figure 9). First of all, the cabin was rectangular, about twenty-five feet long and eighteen feet wide, and oriented approximately northeast–southwest along the rock wall face. The cabin incorporated a large existing granite boulder into its west wall. For the sake of stability the cabin needed four notched corners to support a roof and to sustain a substantial snow load. Accordingly, the cabin must have partially enclosed the rock. Its north and south walls (each approximately eighteen feet long) were north and south of the rock and extended west of the east face of the rock. Two short west walls (approximately four to four and a half feet long) joined the southwest corners of the structure to the rock. The wall ends that abutted the rock probably were unframed. Wedges placed firmly between the wall logs may have been used to hold the logs level and in place. The postholes discovered at the ends of both walls during the 1986 excavation, however, demonstrate that cribbing was used to tie the otherwise floating wall ends to the large rock. Cribbing, a common nineteenth-century log cabin construction method used in such situations, involved driving vertical posts on both sides of horizontally laid wall logs.

By partially encompassing the rock and using its natural curvature and angled face, the westernmost roof log could have been laid almost flush with the face of the rock. A gap of only a few inches would remain, closed enough to keep out snow but open enough to vent smoke up from the fire pit(s). Two prominent notches located about eight feet up on the face of the rock suggest where the roof log was placed. Not only were cabin side walls of seven to eight feet typical of the period, but the height of eight feet also accords well with written accounts suggesting that the Breen cabin was seven to eight feet high and the Graves-Reed cabin was eight to nine feet high.[58]

Perhaps the most controversial aspect of the cabin's reconstruction is the placement of its doorway. Traditionally, the doorway in nineteenth-century American log cabins was placed in the east wall to capture the morning sun. The east wall of the Murphy cabin would have been the side opposite the rock. There is very little archaeological evidence of a doorway anywhere in the cabin site; however, near the northern corner of the east wall is an unusually heavy concentration of glass bottle and tobacco pipe fragments and other refuse. Such a concentration would be expected from the well-known western frontier pattern of throwing trash out of or toward the door away from the main living area. Yet McGlashan's comment that he removed the last log remaining at the cabin in 1893, "the log on the western side of the cabin, the one containing the threshold of the door," appears to contradict such an interpretation.[59] Furthermore, survivor William Murphy's sketch of the cabin, published in Thompson and West's *History of Nevada County, California* (1880), confuses the issue even more by placing the doorway in the north (or northeast) wall.[60] In actuality, however, McGlashan's comment about the log with the threshold may be interpreted as additional evidence that the door was in the east wall. The log could not have been on the west side, since that would place the doorway directly against the rock. McGlashan, therefore, may have intended to refer to the wall opposite the rock, which would have been the east wall.

In addition to the direct archaeological and documentary evidence of how the Murphy cabin was constructed, comparative studies of folk architecture suggest some other details. The double saddle notch, which left the log ends extending only a few inches beyond the plane of the wall, was the simplest and most common way of joining the corners of log cabins. Certainly the members of the Donner party would have been familiar with the technique. Double notching allowed the logs to be fitted closely together, greatly reducing the chinking needed to close gaps in the walls. That this method was used to construct the Graves-Reed cabin is suggested by Bryarly and Geiger's observation in 1849 that "logs were fitted very nicely together, there being scarcely a crevice between."[61] Twigs or small limbs, rocks, pieces of canvas or cloth, or mud probably would have been used for whatever chinking was needed. Bryarly and Geiger also observed that the logs in the Graves-Reed cabin were "from 8 inches to a ft. in diameter";[62] the same log size was probably used at the Murphy cabin, especially given that lodgepole pines of that size are typical of the region. Finally, the logs used to build the cabin probably were left round and covered with bark.

Whatever the physical appearance of the cabin, the space within it was cramped. A typical small log cabin considered suitable for a single individual would have been about sixteen by twenty feet or perhaps a bit larger.[63] As many as ten to fifteen people lived in each of the two sixteen-by-sixteen-foot rooms of the Graves-Reed cabin. The nine people in the Breen cabin lived in an even smaller space, estimated by McGlashan to have been as little as twelve by fourteen feet; and as many as sixteen people lived in the Murphy cabin in a space of eighteen by twenty-five feet.

4 : Archaeology of the Alder Creek Camp

On or about October 25, 1846, the wagons carrying the George and Jacob Donner families, the last of the three groups of the Donner party to leave the Truckee Meadows camp, traveled slowly beside the Truckee River toward the Sierra Nevada. Before long, a broken wagon axle stopped the group. George Donner cut his hand severely during its repair; it was an injury that would make him an invalid. After the delay, the group ran into the same early winter storm that had forced the two forward groups of the Donner company to turn back to Donner Lake and make camp. On or about November 3, 1846, the Donner family contingent camped several miles down the trail from the lake camp. In a letter she wrote to C. F. McGlashan several years later, Leanna C. Donner (then Mrs. John App) recalled, "We had no time to build a Cabin the Snow came on So Sudden that we had barely time to pitch our tent, and put up a small brush shed, as it were. One side open, thus [sketch in letter] this brush Shed was covered with pine boughs, and then covered with Rubber coats, Quilts etc. My uncle Jacob [Donner] & family also had a tent, he camped near us."[1] Who lived in the camp at Alder Creek? Certainly the sixteen members of the George and Jacob Donner families were there; exactly how many others were there as well is unknown. *Ordeal by Hunger*, by George Stewart, places the recently widowed Mrs. Wolfinger and four teamsters (Jean Baptiste Trudeau, James Smith, Samuel Shoemaker, and Joseph Reinhardt) in the camp,[2] giving a total of six men, three women, and twelve children. Joseph A. King's *Winter of Entrapment* adds four more to the roster, all young men traveling alone: John Denton, Noah James, Charles Burger, and Antonio.[3] Both Denton and Burger later moved to the Donner Lake camp, as, probably, did Antonio, who joined the Forlorn Hope escape party in mid-December.

Personal Reminiscences of the Alder Creek Camp

Only a few written accounts provide firsthand glimpses of the Alder Creek camp. Patrick Breen's diary first mentions the camp in the December 17, 1846, entry: "Milt. [Elliott] & Noah [James] went to Donnos 8 days since not returned yet, thinks they got lost in the snow. J. Denton here today."[4] Milt Elliott traveled with the Reed family and lived at the lake camp. Noah James and John Denton traveled with the Donner family and presumably lived at the Alder Creek camp in the beginning; however, the Breen diary makes it quite clear that both had moved to the lake camp by December 17. The December 21 entry from the same diary records that "Milt. got back last night from Donos camp sad news. Jake Donno Sam Shoemaker Rinehart, & Smith are dead the rest of them in a low situation."[5] Just how low is suggested by the reminiscences of Georgia A. Donner, one of George Donner's daughters, about the living conditions at the camp:

> The families shared with one another as long as they had anything to share. Each one's portion was very small. The hides were boiled, and the bones were burned brown and eaten. We tried to eat a decayed buffalo robe, but it was too tough, and there was no nourishment in it. Some of the few mice that came into camp were caught and eaten. Some days we could not keep a fire, and many times during both days and nights, snow was shoveled from off our tent and from around it that we might not be buried alive. Mother remarked one day that it had been two weeks that our beds and clothing upon our bodies had been wet.[6]

Jean Baptiste Trudeau, who traveled with the Donner family, offered another glimpse of the Alder Creek camp years later:

> I belonged to old Mr. Donner's Camp. . . . It was snowing when we stopped, and I told him best to build a hut like the Indians Wigwam with an opening at the top for the smoke to escape. We all helped with the hut. Short posts were driven in the ground on the insides across which sticks were laid, and on them pine boughs were thickly spread This arrangement served as comfortable beds when they could be kept dry.

I cut the wood above the snow, I used to climb the trees to saw off the limbs, and to gather the pine cones to start the fire with. . . . When it rained hard or at night we used to cover the coals and knots, first with ashes, and then put a large camp kettle over them to keep them dry and alive. . . . We were often without fires for days, and meat was beyond reach at times, then we ate the hides, and strings or went hungry; but at no time did the people in the Donner Camps eat human flesh.[7]

Breen's diary documents fairly frequent travel back and forth between the two mountain camps. The January 8, 1847, entry, for example, records "Milt. & Eliza [Williams] going to Donos."[8] Eliza showed up again at the lake camp on January 17, but Milt didn't return until January 21, with frozen toes and news that the "donoughs are all well." Noah James stayed at the Alder Creek camp until he returned to the lake camp on February 21 or 22 with the first rescue expedition, led by Aquilla Glover, and then left with them on the return trip to California. Breen's diary also mentions Jean Baptiste Trudeau's presence at the lake camp on January 21. Trudeau, however, had returned to the Alder Creek camp by February 22 and lived in the Jacob Donner tent until March 13 or 14, when he left for California with the third relief party.

Other firsthand accounts tell of the last days of the camp. Breen's entry for February 26, 1847, describes the Donners' last desperate response to the rapidly deteriorating living conditions: "The Donnos told the California folks [arriving with a relief party] that they [would] commence to eat the dead people 4 days ago, if they did not succeed that day or next in finding their cattle then under ten or twelve feet of snow & did not know the spot or near it, I suppose they have done so ere this time."[9] Not long afterward, James Reed's relief party, the second rescue expedition, arrived at the mountain camps. Reed recorded his impressions of the Alder Creek camp in his diary entry for March 2, 1847:

left early this morning with 3 of the men and went to Donners where Cady & Clark had arrived yesty found all alive cheered [?] them [?] and sent Cady back for more provisions [two words illegible] of any found here but 3 child of J Donner that could com with us at George Donner tent there was 3 Stout harty children his wife was able to travel but preferred to stay with her husband until provision should arrive, which was confidently expected by Comd [?] Woodworth, who was at Cap Suters the day before I left Mr. Johnsons, here I left two of my men Cady & Clark one with each tent to cook and as fast as possible resuscitate the enfeebled so that might in a few days start, took 3 children of J Donner.[10]

An account written by James Reed in 1871 and published in the *Pacific Rural Press* adds another detail about the camp: "We found Mrs. Jacob Donner in a very feeble condition. Her husband had died early in the winter. We removed the tent and placed it in a more comfortable situation. I then visited the tent of Geo. Donner, close by, and found him and his wife."[11]

The next firsthand account of the situation at Alder Creek is from mid-April 1847, when the fourth relief party visited. J. Quinn Thornton recorded some secondhand information based on his interviews with William Eddy late in 1847. Eddy, however, who had survived the Forlorn Hope escape attempt, did not visit the Alder Creek camp and spent only two hours at the lake camp when he returned with the third relief. The interviews suggest that on March 14, 1847, only Tamsen Donner and the dying George Donner remained at the Alder Creek camp.[12] Finally, William Fallon's alleged journal of the fourth relief party, which was printed in the June 5, 1847, issue of the *California Star* but has never been found, includes the following entry for April 17, 1847: "It brought us to the camp of Jacob Donner, where it had evidently left that morning. There we found property of every discription, books, calicoes, tea, coffee, shoes, purcussion caps, household and kitchen furniture scattered in very direction, and mostly in water."[13] The journal continues with a rather gruesome, and perhaps fanciful, description of the butchered remains of the body of George Donner in a large iron kettle in front of the tent. Fallon found no one living in the camp.

In the following years the Alder Creek camp, like the lake camp, had numerous visitors. Among the earliest was the military expedition led by General Stephen Watts Kearny. The diary of Sergeant Nathaniel Jones, who traveled with Kearny's party, mentions that after leaving the lake camp on June 22, 1847, the expedition "started about two in the afternoon came 7 miles and camped. One mile above here was another cabin and more dead bodies, but the General did not order them buried."[14] In September of the same year, Daniel Tyler, traveling with a group of Mormon emigrants, made the following observations:

> During the 3rd of September, we passed other wagons at the place where General Kearney's [*sic*] party had buried the remains of the famished emigrants and at night reached the place where the rear wagons of the unfortunate Hastings company [the Donner party] were blocked by the snow, and were horrified at the sight which met our view—a skull covered with hair lying here, a mangled arm or leg yonder, with the bones broken as one would break a beef shank to obtain the marrow from it; a whole body in another place, covered with a blanket, and portions of other bodies scattered around in different directions.[15]

Emigrant John A. Markle visited the camp on August 20, 1849. He wrote in his diary that the remains of the Alder Creek camp were visible "one or two miles from the road on the right hand side" and that he rode to the camp, where he found "fragments" and "human bones" on the ground.[16]

Where Was the Alder Creek Camp?

The existing documents fail to answer several questions about the Alder Creek camp—questions that archaeological studies are well suited to explore. First is the question of exactly where the campsite is. Given the few firsthand accounts of the Alder Creek camp, it should come as no surprise that there is disagreement over its location. C. F. McGlashan placed the site about five miles northeast of the lake camp on Alder Creek (a tributary of Prosser Creek that then flowed into the Truckee River) based on two visits to the site in 1879, one with Nicholas Clark, a member of the second relief party who spent three weeks at the camp in March 1847, and one with survivor William C. Graves.[17] In 1921 the site was visited by P. M Weddell of San Jose, California, a teacher and Donner party enthusiast who had interviewed McGlashan and received directions to the site from him.[18] Weddell placed wooden signs on trees to mark both the location of the trail taken by the Donner party and the site of the Alder Creek camp. In 1927 Weddell and McGlashan visited the site together, and McGlashan verified the marked location of the camp; Weddell's wooden markers are still in place.[19] Today, the site is part of the Tahoe National Forest, which has developed an interpretative trail and day-use recreational facilities there.

In addition to McGlashan's testimony, Weddell's identification of the campsite is supported by two other sources. First, as already mentioned, the diaries kept by Sergeant Nathaniel Jones, Daniel Tyler, and John A. Markle contain observations about the location of the camp; second, Weddell's identification is also supported by the presence of "tall stumps" of trees cut by the Donner party. In "Location of the Donner Family Camp," Weddell states that "those [trees] cut . . . at the Alder Creek camp left stumps twelve feet high, showing the extent of the snowfall at the head of Alder Creek Valley. . . . There are but two of the old, high stumps now standing. . . . When I began marking this camp and the emigrant trail 20 or more years ago, there were other high stumps in different places within the Alder Creek camp, but they have fallen into decay and disappeared."[20]

The spot marked by Weddell as the site of the Alder Creek camp has not been universally accepted, however, in spite of this evidence. Perhaps the main issue clouding the location of the site is the dispute over the route actually taken by the Donner party.[21] The Truckee River route was pioneered in 1844 by the Stevens-Townsend-Murphy party under the guidance of mountain man Caleb Greenwood, who was following the advice of the Paiute headman Truckee.[22] The route went up Truckee Canyon along the river but proved difficult to traverse.[23] On their return trip east from California the following year, Greenwood and his sons found a detour that avoided the steep segment of the Truckee River Canyon.[24] The detour turned north and left the canyon in the vicinity of what is now the town of Verdi, went around the north end of the Verdi Range through Dog Valley, and then turned southward to cross the Little Truckee, Prosser Creek, and Alder Creek before returning to the Truckee River at about the center of what today is the town of Truckee.

That route appears to have been used by all the emigrant parties traveling the California Trail between 1845 and 1850. John Frémont and Lansford Hastings, traveling separately, used the detour on their way to California in 1845. Hastings also traveled along the route the next year, both on his way east and on his return trip to California just ahead of the Donner party. In addition, Jacob Snyder's 1845 diary and John Markle's 1849 diary strongly suggest that they followed this route.[25] That the Donner party also traveled this road is suggested by a map made from memory by William C. Graves in 1879 and published in Virginia Reed Murphy's *Across the Plains with the Donner Party*. The map shows what appears to be Prosser Creek and Alder Creek running perpendicular to the road taken by the Donner party, which would be expected if the party stuck to the main Dog Valley route. Unfortunately, the Truckee River is not shown on the map, and it is nearly impossible to orient the trail accurately.

If the Donner family contingent camped at the place on Alder Creek identified by McGlashan, however, either they camped far from the main emigrant road or they took a different road. That the camp was not close to the main emigrant road is supported by John Markle's diary account, which, as previously stated, places the camp "one or two miles" away from the road and seven miles from Donner Lake. Undoubtedly taking this into account, Weddell marked the route taken by the Donner party as a dogleg off the main trail. Weddell's route follows the faint traces of an old road still visible today. It leaves the main Dog Valley road at Prosser Creek, turns up Alder Creek to climb six hundred feet over a mountain range, and goes down Trout Creek before meeting the main emigrant road again near Donner Lake.

None of the emigrant diaries suggests such a diversion, however, and Weddell's route opens a Pandora's box of questions. Why would the Donner family depart from the commonly used trail and take a deviant, and more difficult, route that rose an additional several hundred feet over mountainous and difficult terrain when they were already exhausted? But if they took the commonly used route, why did they travel at least a mile off the trail to camp? Some historians have argued, therefore, that the McGlashan-Weddell campsite cannot be the correct site; the actual campsite must be closer to the main emigrant road. Weddell's trail, in fact, may be nothing more than an old logging road. Perhaps the most vociferous proponent of this argument was Edwin H. Johnson, an Oakland, California, lawyer and Donner party enthusiast who contended in the 1940s that he had found the actual campsite to the east of the McGlashan-Weddell site and much closer to the main road. At the site, now submerged by the Prosser Creek Reservoir, he found "the crumbling corner logs of an old cabin, an assortment of old iron kitchen utensils, a stone bordered spot which might be a burial ground and other evidences."[26] Johnson's site seems suspect at first simply because his description of it as the ruins of a "cabin" conflicts with most of the firsthand accounts, which describe the Donner family shelters as "tents" and a "brush shed."[27] On the other hand, the reminiscences of Elitha C. Donner Wilder suggest that the remains of the campsite could have appeared to be cabin ruins: "Uncle and his two men cut logs and cousin Solomon and Will hauled them. Father and I notched them and laid them four logs high, then came the snow. We camped by a tall pine tree, we cut poles and stood them up around the tree and cut brush laid brush around the tree to serve until we could build a house. But the snow came and that was all we had with our tents."[28] The remains of the "four logs high" structure could well be interpreted as a cabin, although there is no evidence in Elitha's account that the log structure was ever completed or used as a domicile, or that it was even in the same place as the brush shelter against the tall pine tree.

Some additional support for Johnson's site location comes from the reminiscences of Mrs. Jennie Calloway Graham Westlow, the stepdaughter of Charles Roberson, who operated the first sawmill on Alder Creek. Mrs. Westlow, who was eighty-one in 1941 and a resident of Sacramento, lived in the Alder Creek area as a child between 1872 and 1880. She recalled finding the ruins of a cabin: "In a tiny glade we found the roofless ruins of an old hut, upon which the willows were encroaching. There was a wagon bed half covered with debris which lay alongside the cabin. Mother, upon seeing the ruin, declared it was one of the Donner shelters. Immediately south of the ruins was a large yellow pine and I believe the tree still stands."[29] They believed the cabin, which was about a quarter of a mile east of the George Donner tree at the McGlashan-Weddell site, to be the Jacob Donner shelter. In August 1941, Mrs. Westlow, Edwin Johnson, and Harry Bagley, a reporter for the *Sacramento Bee*, returned to the area and attempted to locate the remains. The editorial page of the October 19, 1941, issue of the *Oakland Tribune* describes the trip:

> The party turned off the highway between Truckee and Prosser Station and over a rock-studded bumpy road to the old railroad grade to the Norden lumber mill. Three-quarters of a mile up the Alder Creek Valley, near the old railroad crossing they came upon the clump of tamaracks where Johnson, last year, discovered evidences of a cabin. Mrs. Westlow found the place much changed, but, as Bagley writes, a big yellow pine and some tamaracks seemed familiar markings of the spot. Johnson set to

work with an abbreviated hoe and soon unearthed a fragment of rotting
wood. Then other fragments came to light, including a two-foot, crumbling section of a sapling, about five inches in diameter. Imbedded in the
wood were three hand-wrought iron nails. The wagon box could not be
found, however, nor did the area yield any evidence other than the buried
wood and the old nails. And the nails could not be viewed as conclusive
evidence, for the crumbling flume, some fifty yards uphill, had been built
with similar hand wrought nails. "But I am certain the cabin I saw was
near this spot," said Mrs. Westlow. Johnson was elated. A hundred yards to
the north and east is the place where last year he found the crumbling
corner logs of an old cabin, an assortment of old iron kitchen utensils, a
stone bordered spot which might be a burial ground and other evidences
that convinced him he had found a Donner camp site.

Mrs. Westlow returned to Alder Creek in 1943 after reading a newspaper account of a "huge pine tree" being cut in the vicinity of Hobart Mills, a tree that
she remembered as being next to the cabin. She pointed out the cabin ruins,
which included cut nails, to the Truckee Chamber of Commerce.[30]

All in all, the documentary and physical evidence of the camp's location is so
confusing that most authorities leave both alternative routes on reconstruc-
tions of the actual route taken by the Donner party. Harold Curran's *Fearful
Crossing* and Charles Graydon's *Trail of the First Wagons across the Sierra Nevada*, for example, show both routes.[31]

How Many Shelters Were There at the Camp?

Another question that archaeological research may answer involves the number of shelters at the Alder Creek camp. In a letter to C.F. McGlashan dated
April 1, 1879, Leanna Donner App comments about the George Donner family shelter: "I would here state that we had no Cabin. We had no time to build
a Cabin the Snow came on So Sudden that we had barely time to pitch our
tent, and put up a small brush shed, as it were. One side open, thus [sketch in
letter] this brush Shed was covered with pine boughs, and then covered with
Rubber coats, Quilts etc. My Uncle Jacob & family also had a tent, he camped
near us."[32] Later, she recalled in a letter to Eliza Donner Houghton dated November 30, 1902, that "we did not have any hut, our winter quarters were made
of a scaffold, covered with boughs and what few blankets and quilts we could
spare and we had a small tent to sleep in. Our scaffold was built right at the root
of the tree and we cooked under the scaffold."[33]

McGlashan and Weddell marked the site of George Donner's shelter at the
south side of a large pine tree that is still standing at the campsite (Figure 10).
The tree's base, against which, at least according to a popular legend, the

Figure 10: The George Donner tree, looking east toward the most commonly used route of the California Trail, about one mile away and now submerged by Prosser Reservoir. Photograph ©1997 Peter Goin.

Donner family kept a fire going, is scarred with a deep, charred cavity. Such details, factual or legendary, are missing for the Jacob Donner shelter. James Reed also mentioned seeing only the two tents when he visited the camp on March 2, 1847. The widowed Mrs. Wolfinger apparently lived with the George Donner family, but firsthand accounts do not say where the teamsters or the other single men at the camp lived. *Ordeal by Hunger* puts them in a third, "wigwam" shelter across the creek from the Donner family tents.[34] This third shelter, however, while plausible and even likely, is not documented in firsthand accounts. Weddell appears to have marked only the sites of the two Donner family shelters. The number of shelters at the Alder Creek camp—two or three or more—is thus another topic open to different interpretations. To make the matter even more confusing, James Reed's 1871 account of his visit to the camp says that his rescue party moved the Jacob Donner family tent to another place on March 1, 1847, but makes no mention of moving George Donner's tent. If all these accounts are correct, the archaeological remains of at least five shelter sites might be encountered at the Alder Creek camp: George Donner's tent, George Donner's brush shed, Jacob Donner's first tent, Jacob Donner's second tent, and the teamsters' shelter.

How Was the Camp Laid Out?

Yet another mystery about the Alder Creek camp is its layout. The cabins at the lake camp were spread out along Donner Creek for one quarter of a mile, a widely spaced arrangement caused, at least in part, by social dissension within the party. The traditional view of the layout of the Alder Creek camp, however, is quite different. Weddell, for example, marked the locations of the George Donner and the Jacob Donner shelters at the Alder Creek location less than a hundred meters apart. For the most part, this "tightly packed" model of the camp's layout has the best support in written accounts. James Reed's 1871 reminiscences, for example, describe the two shelters as being "close by."[35] Eliza Donner Houghton recalled that her Uncle Jacob's shelter was "not far from us."[36] Leanna Donner App remembered that her Uncle Jacob's shelter was "near us," but later put the distance at "about 300 yards,"[37] spacing that is more like the arrangement at the lake camp. Archaeological evidence may yet resolve the dispute.

On the Archaeological Road Again

In 1989, with the hope of finding answers to the questions asked above, the University of Nevada, Reno, in cooperation with the Tahoe National Forest, began an archaeological study of the spot marked by McGlashan and Weddell as the site of the Donner family camp on Alder Creek. The site lies within the boundaries of a Tahoe National Forest recreation area with an interpretative trail. An effort by the national forest staff to make the trail more accessible to disabled visitors initiated the archaeological investigation. Historic preservation laws and policies required mitigation of the impacts of these trail improvements on areas of historical importance near the reputed site of the Jacob Donner shelter. The mitigation involved a surface reconnaissance and the excavation of several pits to examine what was buried there. Remarkably little, however, came from this humble beginning. The ground yielded only a few basalt flakes and twentieth-century artifacts—certainly nothing suggesting the remains of a mid-1840s emigrant campsite.

During the following summer, 1990, the study, now part of a UNR archaeological field school, focused on the reputed site of the George Donner shelter. Preliminary tree ring studies by dendroecologist Martin Rose of the Desert Research Institute showed the tree marked by McGlashan and Weddell to be six to eight hundred years old. Certainly it was there, and already quite large, at the time of the Donner party tragedy. The UNR students and several volunteers from the local community and elsewhere spent three weeks excavating the area around the tree with small tools (Figures 11, 12). Imagine our disap-

Figure 11: The excavation at the George Donner tree locality in 1990, looking south.

Figure 12: Screening dirt at the George Donner tree excavation, looking east toward Prosser Reservoir.

Figure 13: Pedestrian survey of the Alder Creek campsite in 1990, looking south.

pointment, and the students' boredom, at finding only a few basalt flakes and post-1950s artifacts such as pull tabs from aluminum cans, cigarette butts, and fragments of black plastic. There was no evidence at all that the Donner party had been there. The validity of the McGlashan-Weddell location seemed in jeopardy.

We then devised a new plan. The archaeologists, students, and volunteers in the group would systematically walk over the immediate vicinity of the two marked shelter sites searching for visible evidence of the Alder Creek camp. We set up a checkerboard-like grid that divided the site into twenty-meter-square blocks, and two-person teams walked over each of the blocks in strips, or transects, two meters wide and parallel (Figure 13). Pedestrian, or "walk-over," surveys such as these, however, tell us only what is visible on the ground surface, not what is buried beneath. Buried remains can be found by digging, of course, but remote sensing with electronic instruments can sometimes locate buried objects and eliminate the need for blindly digging up large areas. Three volunteers experienced in the use of metal detectors swept the survey blocks with their instruments in an effort to locate metallic anomalies that might identify buried remains. The detector operators walked parallel transects four feet apart, swinging their instruments in a side-to-side sweeping motion. When a "hot spot" was discovered, archaeologists used trowels or shovels to dig out the object, which they identified and plotted on a site map.

Many of the objects found by the metal detectors were left by twentieth-century visitors. Some, however, clearly date well back into the nineteenth century and could be contemporaneous with the Donner party. The site map showed two artifact clusters: one in a sagebrush zone just southwest of the Weddell-marked George Donner tree, the other in a marshy meadow east and slightly north of the Weddell-marked Jacob Donner shelter. During the remaining two weeks of the 1990 field season, the field school students and volunteers excavated the two clusters. They found many artifacts that can definitely be dated to the Donner party period, including two coins, along with bone and charcoal fragments. To define the boundaries of the two Donner party localities more precisely, the archaeologists returned briefly to the Alder Creek site during the summer of 1992 and excavated several more pits (Figure 14).

The last phase of the archaeological study of the Alder Creek site took place in 1993. As part of the United States Forest Service's "Passport in Time" program, Richard Markley of the Tahoe National Forest brought together a group of twenty-six metal detector enthusiasts from around the country to expand the geographical area covered by the 1990 survey at the site. The group included the three volunteers who did the 1990 survey. Three teams of twelve people each surveyed parallel transects sixteen to eighteen feet wide. Each team included eight or nine people with metal detectors—at least one using a deep-ranging (double box) instrument—and two or three archaeologists. The detectorists walked in a staggered line down the transect, separated by enough distance to prevent electronic interference from neighboring instruments but close enough to overlap their sweeps. As in the 1990 survey, the archaeologists on the teams used trowels or shovels to probe for buried objects located by the metal detectors. Forest Service engineers mapped the location of each object with a GPS (global positioning system) unit and a total station transit. No new artifact clusters datable to the Donner party period were found during the 1993 survey, but the work added to our knowledge of the site environs.

Archaeological Images of the Alder Creek Camp

Table 3 shows the fourteen soil layers and other deposits that make up the archaeological context of the Alder Creek site. The deposits labeled strata I and XI are geographical members of a tan brown silt-loam to fine sandy loam soil covering much of the site to a depth of twenty to thirty-five centimeters and containing a mixture of twentieth-century, nineteenth-century, and earlier artifacts. Bioturbation, mostly rodent activity, has greatly disturbed these deposits in most areas of the site. Below the top deposits are several transitional soil layers. Strata II, X, and XIV are geographical members of a light brown clay-

SITE SURVEY

of the archeological excavations in the
Donner Camp Picnic Area located in the
S.E. 1/4 of the S.E. 1/4 of Section 27,
Township 18 North, Range 16 East
in the unincorporated territory of the
County of Nevada, California

N 140 METERS

N 120 METERS

N 100 METERS

UNIT 3

N 80 METERS

N 60 METERS

N 40 METERS

E 80 METERS

E 60 METERS

E 40 METERS

E 20 METERS

E 0 METERS

W 20 METERS

W 40 METERS

W 60 METERS

W 80 METERS

N 100 METERS

N 80 METERS

N 60 METERS

N 40 METERS

UNIT 1

UNIT 6

UNIT 7

UNIT 2

UNIT 8

UNIT 5

UNITS 29,38,25
UNITS 23,15,37,20
UNIT 4
UNITS 16,27,26,19,40
UNITS 33,14,30,21,31,39
UNITS 34,22,9,12,18
UNITS 17,28,13,24,32,41
UNITS 11,36,10,35,43,42

George Donner Locality

UNITS 63,60
UNITS 64,61
UNIT 70

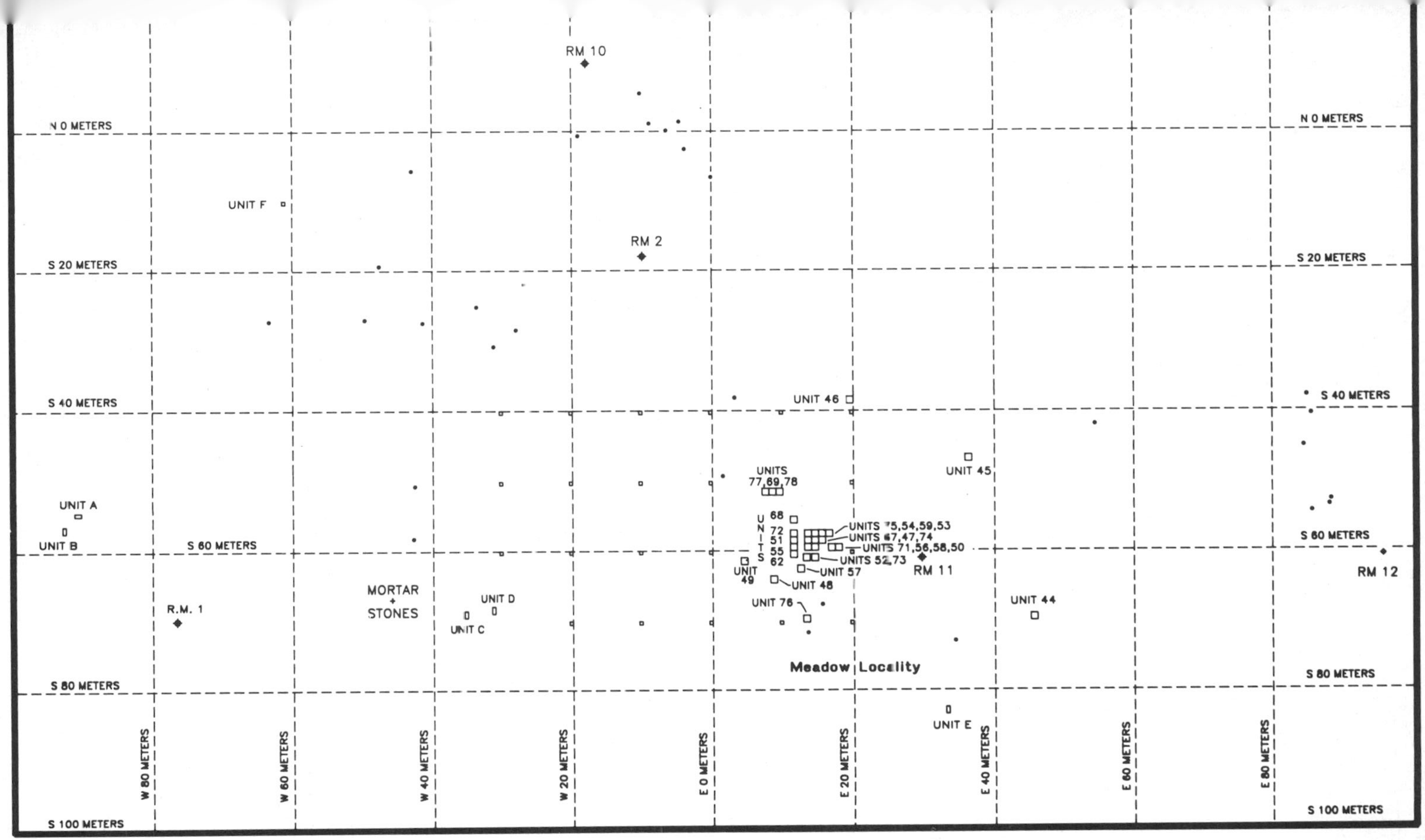

Figure 14: Plan of Alder Creek campsite excavations. Units A–D = test pits excavated in 1989; numbered squares (e.g., Unit 20) = pits excavated in 1990; unnumbered small squares = test pits excavated in 1992; closed circles = artifacts located by metal detector surveys outside excavated areas.

Table 3: The Stratigraphy of the Alder Creek Campsite

Stratum	Depth below Surface	Description
I	0–30 cm	Tan brown; fine sandy loam; unconsolidated; two compact surfaces
II	30–45 cm	Tan brown silt-loam with orange mottling; increased clay content; pebbles to gravel; sandy loam; some grussified rock
III	45+ cm	Wavy boundary with stratum II; yellowish/brown with more orange mottling; dramatic increase in clay; cobbles; more grussified rock; culturally sterile
IV	0–2 cm	Red cinders
V	0–2 cm	Dark gritty veneer directly below stratum IV (possibly pulverized red cinders)
VI	2–3 cm	Compact surface directly below strata I, IV, and V; similar to compact surfaces in stratum I; brown to light gray
VII	2–3 cm	Decomposing cinder and cinder chunks in tightly defined, compact layer
VIII	5–35 cm	Light brown, semidry, unconsolidated silt with grass; pebbles
IX	3–5 cm	Sandy silt, grainy, small pebbles; sandwiched between strata VII and VIII
VIII/X	35–45 cm	Interface between strata VIII and X; no abrupt boundary; transitional stratum with the same soil composition
X	45+ cm	Yellowish brown silt-loam with increased clay; some cobbles; gravel; older than 25,000 years B.P.
XI	0–20 cm	Dark brown loose silt-loam in some places, tan/orange compact silt-loam in others; pebbles; roots; extensive rodent disturbance
XII	20–30 cm	Dark brown/gray; cobbles to rock; increased clay
XIII	20–35 cm	Same as stratum XI but with orange mottling (rust stains); increased clay content; not present everywhere and most prevalent in westernmost meadow; weathering layer of stratum XIV
XIV	30+ cm	Tan/brown; no orange mottling; increased clay; contains a few basalt flakes

loam to clay soil layer with orange mottling that underlies all of the other deposits at the site and contains only a few prehistoric lithic artifacts. The layer appears to be at least twenty-five thousand years old.

The Jacob Donner Locality

The 1989 excavation at the site marked by McGlashan and Weddell as the Jacob Donner shelter revealed nothing left by the Donner party. Excavators found only twentieth-century artifacts and basalt flakes that are most likely of Native American origin. Three stratified layers or deposits form the archaeological context of the site. The topmost layer, stratum XI, contains twentieth-century artifacts. Just below it is stratum XIII, a transitional layer that lies on top of and appears to be a weathered zone of stratum XIV, a light brown clay-loam layer that extends throughout the southern edge of the Alder Creek campground. Strata XIII and XIV contain a few basalt flakes, probably from earlier Native American occupation of the region, but no other artifacts.

The George Donner Locality

The George Donner tree locality excavated in 1990 yielded several distinct soil layers or other deposits. Each of these was excavated separately, but no artifacts or other physical remains that could be tied to the Donner party came to light. The topmost layers (strata I, IV, and V) contain a few basalt flakes from the manufacture of Native American stone tools, also scattered throughout the site down to a depth of sixty to seventy centimeters, along with a few artifacts of twentieth-century origin such as black plastic fragments, aluminum foil, peanut shells, cigarette butts, and .22 cartridge casings. Thin layers of intact or pulverized red cinders (strata IV and V) cover most of the existing ground surface on the west side of the tree. The Forest Service probably deposited the red cinders within the last thirty or forty years to prepare a more durable surface for visitors to the tree. Below this, stratum I, the fine, sandy loam covering the ground surface over most of the site, replaces the cinders. On the east side of the tree, an area that grades into a marshy meadow, stratum I extends downward more than thirty-five centimeters before being replaced by clay.

Below these surface layers, the stratigraphy is more complex. Stratum VI, a compacted sandy loam deposit, occurs next in the profiles exposed by the excavated pits on the west side of the tree. Below that is what appears to be a transition from an unconsolidated sandy loam with small pebbles to a more consolidated sandy clay-loam with cobbles and large gravel. In most of the excavated pits, the transition begins with stratum VII and continues through strata VIII, IX, and VIII–IX. Below a depth of forty to fifty centimeters, the geological deposits in the locality change to stratum X, a yellowish brown silt-loam layer with more clay, cobbles, and gravel that the late geoarchaeologist Jonathan Davis estimated to be more than twenty-five thousand years old. All of the layers that we examined contained a few basalt flakes down to a depth of nearly sixty-five centimeters but no other artifacts.

Despite its early promise, the excavation at the George Donner tree revealed no material remains of the Donner party episode. Two characteristics of the tree seem to have contributed to its past interpretation as the location of the George Donner shelter: the age and size of the tree and the charred cavity on the west side. The tree certainly is old enough and large enough to have been used as part of the shelter; however, several other trees in the general area appear to be equally large and ancient. Perhaps the most convincing evidence to many people is the charred cavity on the west side of the tree. Similar cavities, however, are found on several of the other surviving large and old trees in the area, and most of them have the same charring. In fact, the charring probably is the result of forest fires.

The Meadow Locality

The largest of the two artifact clusters located by the 1990 metal detector survey were in the meadow east of the Jacob Donner shelter. Probes of the buried deposits turned up many artifacts and other material remains of Donner party vintage. Later in the 1990 field season, the excavation was expanded to include a total of twenty-eight one-meter-square pits. In 1992, archaeologists dug another twenty-one pits, each fifty centimeters square, at the locality to define its boundaries more precisely. The archaeological context of the artifacts and other material remains at the meadow locality includes strata XI, XIII, and XIV.

At the top is stratum XI, a thick layer of loosely to densely packed dark brown to tan-orange silt-loam that covers the locality from the surface down to a depth of about twenty centimeters. The layer has been churned extensively by rodents, some of which were encountered in the layer during the course of the 1990 excavation. Artifacts found in the stratum include lead balls, fragments of ceramic tableware and glass bottles, cut nails, and woodworking tools that date to the Donner party period. In addition the deposit contains highly dispersed and fragmented burned bone, ash, and charcoal. Artifacts and other refuse left by domestic activities were found throughout the layer, which has been badly bioturbated by rodent activity, but no hearths or concentrated lenses of bone and ash that would confirm this locality as the remains of one of the shelters were located.

Next down in the stratigraphic sequence is stratum XIII, a layer of tan or light brown clay-silt loam with orange mottling. The layer reflects a transition to,

Figure 15: The anthill stump locality, looking east.

and may have been caused by the weathering of, stratum XIV, which lies at the bottom of the sequence and is the local geographical member of the deep deposit that underlies all of the Alder Creek site. Neither stratum contains artifacts other than a few basalt flakes.

The abundant archaeological remains recovered from the meadow locality suggest the kinds of domestic activities that would have taken place at a shelter occupied by one of the Donner families. Indeed, the remains are quite similar to those found at the site of the Murphy cabin and include fragments of ceramic tableware and glass bottles, lead balls, charcoal and ash, charred and calcined bone fragments, and buttons that date to the Donner party period. The site is difficult to interpret, however, because of the extensive disturbance and mixing of the soil matrix by rodents. Furthermore, the excavators found no hearth or fire pit, which would provide the best evidence that a shelter had once occupied the spot.

The Anthill Stump Locality

The second cluster of Donner party–era artifacts found by the metal detector sweeps in 1990 is at a decaying tree stump with an anthill southwest of the George Donner tree locality (Figure 15). Archaeologists probing with trowels found several buried artifacts of Donner party vintage. They then expanded the excavation to include a total of seven one-meter-square test units. In 1992, archaeologists dug another eight pits at the locality, each a fifty-centimeter square, to more precisely define its boundaries. Two layers or deposits form the archaeological context of the site. At the top is stratum I, an unconsolidated layer of tan brown sandy loam that extends from the surface downward to a depth of about forty centimeters. In addition to several basalt flakes and other lithic debitage of early Native American origin, the excavators found two 1830s coins, percussion caps, lead balls, cut nails, and other artifacts dating to the Donner party period in the layer. Below this is stratum II, a more consolidated layer of sandy clay-loam containing cobbles and large gravel. Basalt flakes but no other artifacts were found in the layer down to a depth of about sixty centimeters.

The anthill stump excavation revealed little archaeological evidence of domestic activity. No bone, charcoal, ceramic tableware, glass bottles, or other domestic artifacts were found. The artifact assemblage includes several cut nails and tacks, percussion caps, lead balls, a pewter coat button, and two 1830s coins that date to the Donner party period, but nothing about the archaeological remains suggests that this is the site of one of the shelters. The artifacts in this cluster are probably just some of the trash that William "LeGros" Fallon observed to be widely scattered around the camp, and may indicate the spot where a wagon once stood.[38]

Isolated Artifacts

The pedestrian survey and metal detector sweeps of the McGlashan-Weddell site turned up several isolated artifacts in addition to the clusters at the meadow and anthill stump localities. Most of the isolated artifacts are buttons, nails, lead balls or other firearms-related items, hand tools (e.g., wood bits from a bit and brace, a masonry bit for a hand auger, a flat bastard file, and an iron wedge), wagon hardware, or animal husbandry hardware. Among the wagon parts are wagon box staples, an iron axle ring, a flat piece of strap-iron, a brass hook with a threaded end that may have been attached to a wagon box, and several wrought carriage nails with clinched ends that may have been used in construction of the wagon box. Artifacts related to animal husbandry include several horseshoe nails, harness buckles, ox shoes, and horseshoes. Other isolated artifacts found at the site include personal items such as jewelry (a ring), table utensils, a military emblem, and a clay tobacco pipe. The military emblem, a brass American eagle with a shield holding arrows (Figure 16), appears to be part of a United States army uniform insignia "worn on the Infantry dress shako from 1821 to 1851 and on the 1855 Light Artillery dress shako, until 1872."[39] Some of the isolated artifacts clearly date to the twentieth century, well after the Donner party, but many are quite consistent with the period of the tragedy.

Figure 16: Brass military emblem found at the Alder Creek campsite.

Is the McGlashan-Weddell Site the Right Place?

Having examined the archaeological evidence, let us now return to the three questions asked at the beginning of the chapter: Where was the Alder Creek camp? How many shelters were at the camp? How was the camp laid out? Of these, the archaeological evidence best answers the question of whether or not the McGlashan-Weddell site is where the Donner family camped on Alder Creek. The preponderance of the archaeological evidence says yes. The other two questions, however, remain unanswered. The site of one of the shelters may have been found at the meadow locality, but the absence of a hearth or dense charcoal deposits puts even that interpretation in jeopardy.

The archaeological evidence that the Donner family camped at the McGlashan-Weddell site includes the artifacts found at the McGlashan-Weddell site that date to the Donner party period and reflect the kind of activities expected to have taken place at the camp. The ceramic tableware fragments from the meadow locality, for example, are typical of the 1830s–1840s (see Appendix 2). Among them are fragments of sprig-painted cups and saucers probably purchased in the early 1840s. Some of the olive green glass bottle fragments from the same locality are from pictorial whiskey flasks, which were popular during the Donner party period, and from cathedral pickle or food bottles. Clothing buttons found at the site include a button from a greatcoat or vest dating to the 1700s or early 1800s and a button from breeches dating before 1830. The percussion caps from the anthill locality and the large number of lead balls scattered at the site are also consistent with the Donner party period.

Without question, the most exciting artifacts that date to the Donner party period are the two coins: a United States one-cent coin with a Liberty head,

Figure 17: United States liberty penny dated 1830 from the Alder Creek campsite.

Figure 18: Isle of Man farthing dated 1839 from the Alder Creek campsite.

bearing the inscription "Liberty 1830" and a deep dent in its center, perhaps from being struck by a bullet (Figure 17); and a copper farthing from the Isle of Man (between England and Ireland) minted in 1839 (Figure 18). The penny is older, but the farthing is the more intriguing. Its inscriptions read "Victoria Dei Gratia 1839" on one side and "Quocunque ieceris Stabit," the motto of the Isle of Man, on the other.[40] Any of the Donner party members at the Alder Creek camp or anyone from one of the rescue parties could have left the penny; the farthing, however, is another matter. Perhaps it was carried by John Denton, who traveled overland with the George Donner family, the only person in the Donner party known to have come from England.[41] In her reminiscences, Virginia Reed Murphy describes him as being about thirty years old and a gunsmith and gold-beater from Sheffield, England.[42] What connection he had with the Isle of Man—if any—is unknown.

The alternative sites for the Alder Creek camp suggested long ago by Edwin Johnson and Mrs. Jennie Westlow, which are farther to the east and closer to the main emigrant trail, are now submerged by Prosser Reservoir and remain unexamined. In the absence of an archaeological study they cannot be discounted totally as the correct location of the Donner family camp, but that seems unlikely. The preponderance of the existing archaeological evidence strongly supports the McGlashan-Weddell site as the location where the two Donner families and their companions camped during the winter of 1846–1847.

5 : Donner Party Baggage

The baggage carried by overland emigrants to California and Oregon represented the material world of its owners—a world that was on the eve of transformation by a new economic system and new technologies. Although most consumer items were still created at home in the 1840s, large-scale factory production was beginning to put new and cheaper commodities in the marketplace.[1] The Civil War accelerated the flow of factory-made goods, and by the beginning of the Victorian period (1876–1915) the availability of mass-produced commodities had revolutionized and redefined the American way of life.[2] The baggage carried by the Donner party reflected everyday life in America in the mid-1840s—less than two decades before the Civil War—and was, in a sense, a time capsule. Certainly it can tell us much about the lives of the early overland emigrants.

What baggage did the Donner party carry? Written accounts do not give a detailed inventory. In *The Plains Across*, however, historian John Unruh describes what the overland emigrants commonly took with them to California and Oregon, and from that we can guess what the Donner party brought and what happened to it on the way to California.[3] An inventory of the Donner party's baggage must include the things they had with them at the beginning of the trip (things purchased before the trip plus family heirlooms and other possessions), things acquired through exchange with other members of the emigrant party, things acquired at trail trading posts, and things acquired from mobile traders along the trail. To these must be added things acquired by trade with Indians encountered along the way or by vandalizing Indian graves.

Beginning the Journey

Before leaving, the overland emigrants prepared both their wagons and their belongings for the journey. The wagons, usually new, often were crafted especially for the journey; the "Pioneer Palace" of the James Reed family is a good example. Virginia Reed Murphy described the now-famous and controversial wagon in her memoir, "Across the Plains in the Donner Party" (1846) as follows:

> It was what might be called a two-story wagon or "Pioneer palace car," attached to a regular immigrant train. . . . The entrance was on the side, like that of an old-fashioned stage coach, and one that stepped into a small room, as it were, in the centre of the wagon. At the right and left were spring seats with comfortable seats of a Concord coach. In this little room was placed a tiny sheet-iron stove, whose pipe, running through the top of the wagon, was prevented by a circle of tin from setting fire to the canvas cover. A board about a foot wide extended over the wheels on either side the full length of the wagon, thus forming the foundation for a large and roomy second story in which were placed our beds.[4]

Emigrants either purchased the items they wanted to take with them before they set out or brought along family possessions they did not want to leave behind. Each wagon could carry between 2,000 and 5,000 pounds of provisions and equipment.[5] Guidebooks recommended that emigrants carry 200 pounds of flour or meal, 150 pounds of bacon, 10 pounds of coffee, 20 pounds of sugar, and 10 pounds of salt.[6] In *The California Trail*, George R. Stewart notes that a contemporary list of items recommended for a typical overland wagon included "knife, whetstone, ax, hammer, hatchet, spade, saw, gimlet, scissors, needles, palm and pricker (for sewing canvas), last, awls, nails, tacks, pins, thread, wax, twine, shoe leather and pegs, staples, ropes, whip-thongs, cotton cloth, beeswax and tallow, soap, candles, opodeldoc (a linament), herbs, medicines, spyglass, lantern, patent-leather drinking cups, washbowl, and campstool."[7]

On the Trail

The baggage loaded at the beginning of the journey did not remain intact. Some things were used up or discarded, and new things were acquired along the way. In fact, the emigrant party was a kind of "traveling marketplace" whose proprietors bought, sold, bartered, or gave away goods.[8] Most emigrants brought along far too many nonconsumable items that later had to be disposed of; and many ran out of food, which had to be purchased from other emigrants.

Exchanges within the Donner party also took the form of promissory notes, collateral, and verbal agreements to reciprocate once the journey ended in California. In a letter written to C. F. McGlashan in 1879, for example, Patty Reed Lewis relates how her mother was forced by Patrick Dolan to put up "security" in exchange for badly needed cattle for haulage.[9] Exchange with other party members was not the only source of food and supplies, however; the emigrants could also obtain goods and services from several trading posts along the trail. Fur trading companies established the earliest of these—Fort Hall, Fort Boise, and what later became Fort Laramie—in the 1830s. By the early 1840s, the trading posts available to the overland emigrants also included the Robidoux family's post at Scott's Bluff, Fort Bernard, Fort Platte, Fort Bridger, and Fort Smith. Trading posts typically carried such consumables as flour, sugar, coffee, and liquor; durable goods such as iron; livestock; and offered services such as blacksmithing. Fort Bridger, for example, was built in 1841 and by 1842 was servicing overland emigrants with a small store, a blacksmith shop, and a supply of iron.[10]

After 1841, mobile traders, typically from Taos, sold horses, mules, and a variety of other products to emigrant parties along the trail. Unruh notes that "traders up from Taos and Bent's Fort on the Arkansas River added to the 1846 trading possibilities at Fort Bernard and Fort Bridger. At the former they marketed mules and flour; at the latter, dressed buckskins in the form of moccasins, shirts, and pants."[11] James F. Reed, in fact, mentions an encounter with mobile traders at Fort Bridger in his memoir of the journey.[12] Native Americans also engaged the overland emigrants in trade. In a letter written to a cousin in Illinois on May 16, 1847, after reaching California, Virginia Reed mentions a buffalo robe that may have been acquired in this way.[13] In addition to trade, at least one member of the Donner party may have obtained Native American artifacts by looting graves. William Eddy, for example, accused Lewis Keseberg of looting a Sioux burial site on the plains.[14]

Loss and abandonment were other factors that affected baggage. Even today the traces of artifacts simply tossed out along the trail are clearly visible. Written accounts of the Donner party's trip across the Great Salt Lake Desert and the Humboldt Sink document the loss of heavy and bulky artifacts, including household furniture and boxes of books. Sometime between August 31 and September 2, 1846, the Donner party abandoned four wagons in the Great Salt Lake Desert and buried a large cache of goods. The latter may have been found and looted in the early part of the twentieth century.[15] Archaeological excavations conducted by the Utah State Historical Society in the 1980s documented the site (see the Introduction).[16] The Donner party abandoned additional personal belongings along the Humboldt River in early October.

Baggage in the Mountain Camps

Whatever baggage still remained when the Donner party finally arrived in the two mountain camps, then, reflected acquisitions, exchanges, losses, and abandonments along the trail. Patrick Breen's diary of the ordeal in the mountain camps, written between November 20, 1846, and March 1, 1847, gives a glimpse of what the party still carried at this point. The diary mentions an ax, a rifle gun, and tobacco, along with the following personal effects of Charles Burger, who died on the night of December 29, 1846: "money $1.50 two good looking silver watches one razor 3 boxes [percussion] caps. Keysburg took them into his possession. Spitzer took his coat & waistcoat Keysburg all his other effects gold pin one shirt and tools for shavcing."[17] The best known of the Donner party artifacts to survive the ordeal is the wooden doll that Martha (Patty) Reed brought with her when she came down out of the mountains with James Reed's rescue expedition; the Sutter's Fort museum in Sacramento still has the doll.[18]

Acquisitions and losses continued to modify the Donner party's baggage during the winter encampment. Some supplies, for example, were brought to the mountain camps by the relief parties sent from California. The Fort Sutter Papers mention that shirts, trousers, stockings, blankets, buffalo robes, flour, cloth, matches, tobacco, and a jar of mixed pickles were carried to the stranded emigrants by the relief parties.[19] How many such items actually arrived cannot be determined. In addition, the relief parties took some of these supplies back with them—or intended to—when they left. For example, the coverlet wrapped around John Denton when he was left behind in the mountains on one of the return trips had been brought by rescuers.[20]

The fourth relief party, led by William O. Fallon, had a significantly different and greater impact on the Donner party baggage in the mountain camps. It was, in fact, a salvage expedition, sent to collect whatever could be saved in the rapidly melting snow. The entry for April 17, 1847, in Fallon's alleged journal (which was never found but was published in the California Star on June 5, 1847) describes finding "property of every discription, books, calicoes, tea, coffee, shoes, purcussion caps, household and kitchen furniture scattered in every direction" at the Jacob Donner camp.[21] The same journal entry also mentions a bundle that Fallon claims Lewis Keseberg stole from the Alder Creek camp. It contained "silks and jewelry, which had been taken from the camp of the Donners, and amounting in value to about $200; on his [Keseberg's] person they discovered a brace of pistols, recognized to be those of Geo. Donner, and while taking something concealed in his waistcoat, which on being opened was found to be $225 in gold."[22] Finally, the journal entry for April 20 records that the members of the Fallon party "all started for Bear River Valley with packs of 100 cwt. each,"[23] which presumably contained the goods salvaged from the two mountain camps.

The last survivor of the tragedy left on April 21, 1847, but the baggage that was left behind in the mountain camps did not remain undisturbed. Within a short time, the Breens, at least, appear to have returned for their belongings. In a later sketch of the Breen family, for example, Harry J. Breen, a grandson of Patrick Breen, relates that "all the family arrived safely at Sutter's Fort in March 1847, where they rested and retrieved their wagons and possessions from Donner Lake. My father [Edward] and one of his brothers went back over the mountains with the men who brought the wagons over."[24] On June 22 of the same year, General Stephen Watts Kearny and his military detachment passed through the lake camp and buried skeletal remains that they found around one of the cabins.[25] Other emigrant parties traveling along the California Trail between 1847 and 1865 not only observed the remains of the camps but also collected relics.[26] On August 22, 1849, for example, Vincent Geiger and Wakeman Bryarly passed by the Graves-Reed cabin and observed "piles of bones around, but most of cattle, although I did find some half dozen human ones of different parts. . . . Several small stockings were found which still contained the bones of the leg and foot. Remnants of old clothes, with pieces of boxes, stockings and bones in particular, was all that was left to mark that it had once been inhabited."[27] After the transcontinental railroad was completed in 1869, daytrippers from San Francisco visited the mountain camps to picnic and collect relics. C. F. McGlashan dug at the sites of the Breen-Schallenberger cabin and the Graves-Reed cabin in 1879 and removed more of the remaining baggage.

The artifacts found by the University of Nevada, Reno, excavators at the Murphy cabin and the Alder Creek campsite, then, represent not only what the Donner party members had with them at the beginning of the journey but also a complex history of acquisitions, exchanges, abandonments, and losses along the trail and at the camps. Nevertheless, the archaeological remains give an up-close glimpse of the material world of the Donner party that is available from no other source. The remainder of this chapter describes in detail the ceramic tableware and teaware, table utensils, glassware, firearms, clothing and other personal gear, tobacco pipes, hand tools, and wagon hardware recovered from the sites of the two mountain camps.

Ceramic Tableware and Teaware

The Donner party carried many items intended for their new households in California, and it is thus not surprising that many of the artifacts found at the two mountain camps are the remains of domestic goods such as ceramic table-ware and kitchenware, table and kitchen utensils, furniture, mirrors, and writing paraphernalia. Ceramic tableware, more durable than many of the items carried by the party, makes up a significant part of the mountain camps' artifact assemblage.

C. F. McGlashan's early excavation at the site of the Breen cabin at the lake camp turned up "numerous pieces of old porcelain and china-ware. These fragments are readily distinguished by painted flowers, or unique designs enameled in red, blue, or purple colors upon the pure white ground-surface of the china-ware. . . . Among the porcelain are pieces of pretty cups and saucers, and dainty, expensive plates, which in those days were greatly prized."[28] He either did not find ceramics at the site of the Graves-Reed cabin or did not mention them in his recollections of the dig.[29] When the Murphy cabin site was excavated by the UNR team, only four fragments of ceramic tableware were found (Table 4). Of these, one is from what appears to be a whiteware plate decorated with a red transfer-printed design (Figure 19), and another is part of a handle from an undecorated whiteware cup. A strap handle from a green glazed stoneware jug is the only other identifiable ceramic fragment found at the site.

The tableware remains from the Alder Creek campsite are much more abundant. Ceramics specialist George L. Miller kindly consented to examine the collection and reached several conclusions (see Appendix 2). First, he found the tableware to be typical of the 1830s–1840s (Table 5). Most of the collection consists of decorated whiteware, the cheapest decorated tableware available at the time. No plain or undecorated creamware, which would have been cheaper, was found at the campsite. The collection includes plates, cups, saucers, and bowls. All of the plate fragments, from a minimum of two complete plates, are from unscalloped blue shell-edged plates with simple, shallow molded repetitive patterns (Figure 20). The cups and saucers are sprig painted—i.e., they have small flower sprigs with a lot of open white space in between (Figure 21). Sprig painting was used first on French porcelain in the mid-1830s, then adopted by the Staffordshire potters on their earthenwares in the early 1840s. Most likely the sprig-painted cups, saucers, and bowls found at the Alder Creek site were purchased in the early 1840s, or possibly just before the trip west.

Table Utensils

Table utensils were among the more than five hundred artifacts that McGlashan reported finding during his nineteenth-century excavations of the Breen and the Graves-Reed cabin sites: "There are spoons which are bent and rust-eaten, some of which are partially without bowls, and some destitute of han-

Table 4: Ceramic Tableware from the Murphy Cabin Site

Catalog No.	Quantity	Element	Fabric	Decoration
P-612-146/4	1	Plate body (?)	Whiteware	Red transfer printed
P-612-101/1	1	Cup handle	Whiteware	Undecorated
P-612-65/	1	Unknown	Whiteware	Unknown
P-612-17	1	Jug strap	Stoneware	Green glazed

Table 5: Ceramic Tableware from the Alder Creek Campsite

Catalog No.	Qty	Element	Fabric	Decoration
92-11-59	2	Cup rim	Whiteware	Unknown
92-11-68	1	Cup rim	Whiteware	Unknown
92-11-241	1	Cup rim	Whiteware	Unknown
92-11-340	1	Bowl	Whiteware	Sprig painted
92-11-345	1	Cup rim	Whiteware	Undecorated
92-11-363	1	Bowl/cup	Whiteware	Sprig painted
92-11-559	1*	Cup base	Whiteware	Sprig painted
92-11-560				
92-11-222				
92-11-600	1	Bowl rim	Whiteware	Unknown
92-11-624	1	Hollow ware	Whiteware	Blue paint
92-11-746	1	Cup rim	Whiteware	Unknown
92-11-760	1	Cup (?) rim	Whiteware	Unknown
92-11-819	1	Bowl or cup	Whiteware	Sprig paint
92-11-607	1	Saucer	Whiteware	Sprig paint
92-11-608	1	Saucer rim	Whiteware	Undecorated
92-11-20	1	Plate	Whiteware	Blue shell edged
92-11-183	1	Plate/muffin	Whiteware	Blue shell edged
92-11-171	1	Plate/muffin	Whiteware	Blue shell edged
92-11-217	1	Plate/muffin	Whiteware	Blue shell edged
92-11-221	1	Plate/muffin	Whiteware	Blue shell edged
92-11-264	1	Plate/muffin	Whiteware	Blue shell edged
92-11-281	1	Plate/muffin	Whiteware	Blue shell edged
92-11-605	1	Plate/muffin	Whiteware	Blue shell edged
92-11-608	1	Plate/muffin	Whiteware	Blue shell edged
92-11-612	1	Plate/muffin	Whiteware	Blue shell edged
92-11-770	1	Plate/muffin	Whiteware	Blue shell edged
92-11-794	2	Plate/muffin	Whiteware	Blue shell edged
92-11-61	1	Footring	Pearlware	Unknown
92-11-304	1	Footring	Whiteware	Unknown
92-11-764	1	Footring	Whiteware	Unknown
92-11-738	1	Footring	Whiteware	Unknown

*three cross-mended sherds

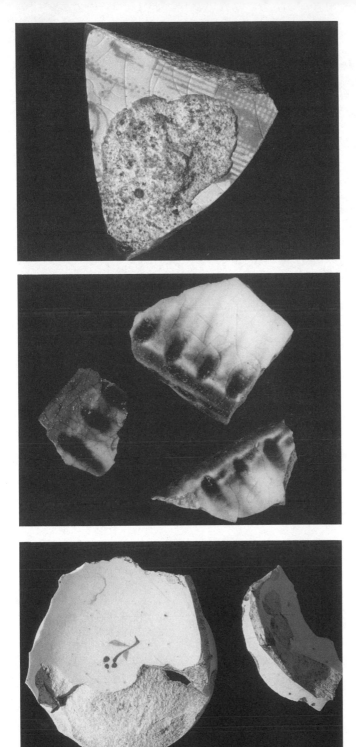

Figure 19: *(top)* Red transfer-printed whiteware from the Murphy cabin site.
Figure 20: *(center)* Blue shell-edged whiteware from the Alder Creek campsite.
Figure 21: *(bottom)* Sprig-painted cup from the Alder Creek campsite.

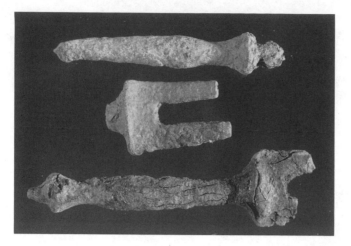

Figure 22: Table utensils from the Alder Creek campsite.

dles, the missing portions being vaguely shadowed in the rust-stained earth in which they were imbedded. Knives there are whose blades are mere skeleton outlines of what they formerly were, and which in some instances appear to be only thin scales of rust. The tines of forks are sometimes pretty well preserved, sometimes almost entirely worn away by the action of rust."[30] Table 6 lists the table utensils found by the excavators at Alder Creek and the Murphy cabin site. The identifiable utensils include brass or other cuprous metal spoons and two-pronged forks constructed from a ferrous metal (Figure 22). In addition, what appears to be the bowl of a crudely carved wooden spoon was found at the site of the Murphy cabin.

Glassware

In his nineteenth-century excavation at the Breen cabin McGlashan found "bits of glassware such as tumblers, vials, and dishes."[31] The Alder Creek and Murphy cabin excavations also turned up fragments of glass containers. Olive Jones, a material culture analyst with the Canadian Parks Service in Ottawa, examined the glass assemblage from the Alder Creek site and identified several bottle or flask fragments that are compatible with the Donner party period (Table 7). Cathedral pickle or food jars contributed the largest number of glass bottle fragments to the Alder Creek assemblage. Pictorial flasks, which were popular during the Donner party period, were identified among the olive green glass bottle fragments found at the site but could not be further identified or fitted together.[32] In addition to these, the glass containers found at Alder Creek included a few aqua medicine vials, an olive green wine or beer bottle, and an aqua flange-lipped bottle.

Table 6: Table Utensils from the Two Mountain Camps

Catalog No.	Site	Type	Material	Decoration
P-612-220/2	Murphy cabin	Spoon	Wood	None
P-612-100/9-2	Murphy cabin	Spoon	Cuprous metal	None
P-612-225	Murphy cabin	Spoon	Cuprous metal	None
92-11-360	Alder Creek	Fork, 2-prong	Ferrous metal	None
92-11-328	Alder Creek	Fork, 2-prong	Ferrous metal	None
92-11-440	Alder Creek	Utensil handle	Ferrous metal	None

In addition to fragments of glass containers similar to those uncovered at Alder Creek, the Murphy cabin excavators found cobalt blue bottles (Table 8). Cobalt blue glassware was used commonly in the late eighteenth and nineteenth centuries for salt dishes, decanters, and medicine and cosmetics containers.[33] Most of the thirty-seven blue glass fragments in the Murphy cabin assemblage appear to have come from octagonal medicine or cosmetics containers.

Firearms

Artifacts related to the ignition systems and ammunition of firearms dominated the material found at the mountain camps. Emigrant parties in the 1840s typically carried the plains or mountain rifle such as the Hawken or Henry,[34] large-caliber—often in the .50–.60 caliber range—muzzle loaders with a patched round ball. Written accounts of a "rifle gun"[35] plus a Hawken rifle presently in the possession of the California Department of Parks and Recreation that is said to have come from the lake camp suggest that the Donner party carried one or both types.

Excavators found the remains of both flintlock and percussion cap firearms at the two mountain camps. The percussion lock, or caplock, which was developed between 1807 and 1816 and was in common use by 1825, was the best of the ignition systems for muzzle loaders.[36] The military adopted the percussion cap system between 1840 and 1845. Percussion cap firearms, therefore, were readily available to the Donner party, and written accounts indicate that some members of the party carried them. The diary of Patrick Breen, for example, refers to "3 boxes caps" among the personal effects of Charles Burger, one of the residents of the Donner Lake camp who perished.[37] C. P. Russell describes the percussion cap in *Guns on the Early Frontier:*

> The cap itself is made of thin-gauge copper. It is slightly conical with a flaring rim around the open end. Four slits extend halfway from the rim toward the dome of the cap, assuring ready and secure adjustment of

Table 7: Glassware from the Alder Creek Campsite

Catalog No.	Element	Type	Color	Marks	Qty
92-11-117	Body	Pictorial flask	Olive green	Molded rib/pictorial	1
92-11-173	Body	Pictorial flask	Olive green	Molded ribbing	1
92-11-100	Body	Pictorial flask	Olive green	Molded pictorial	1
92-11-111	Body	Pictorial flask	Olive green	Molded rib/"S"	1
92-11-3	Body	Pictorial flask	Olive green	Molded pictorial	1
92-11-114	Body	Pictorial flask	Olive green	Molded pictorial	1
92-11-177	Body	Pictorial flask	Olive green	Molded ribbing	1
92-11-387	Body	Pictorial flask	Olive green	Molded ribbing	1
92-11-16	Body	Pictorial flask	Olive green	Molded pictorial	1
92-11-186	Base	Medicine vial	Aqua	Open pontil	1
92-11-401	Shoulder/neck	Cylindrical wine/beer	Olive green	None	1
92-11-848	Base	Medicine vial	Aqua	Open pontil	1
92-11-180	Lip	Unknown	Aqua	Flanged	1
92-11-847	Base/kickup	Unknown	Aqua	Open pontil	1
92-11-754	Base/kickup	Unknown	Aqua	None	1
92-11-65	Body	Cathedral pickle/food	Aqua	Molded ribbing	4
92-11-776	Body	Cathedral pickle/food	Aqua	Molded ribbing	8
92-11-385	Body	Cathedral pickle/food	Aqua	Molded ribbing	1

92-11-773	Body	Cathedral pickle/food	Aqua	Molded ribbing	3
92-11-792	Body	Cathedral pickle/food	Aqua	Molded ribbing	1
92-11-817	Body	Cathedral pickle/food	Aqua	Molded ribbing	1
92-11-49	Body	Cathedral pickle/food	Aqua	Molded ribbing	1
92-11-628	Body	Cathedral pickle/food	Aqua	Molded ribbing	1
92-11-790	Body	Cathedral pickle/food	Aqua	Molded ribbing	2
92-11-809	Body	Cathedral pickle/food	Aqua	Molded ribbing	4
92-11-33	Body	Cathedral pickle/food	Aqua	Molded ribbing	3
92-11-80	Body	Cathedral pickle/food	Aqua	Molded ribbing	1
92-11-64	Body	Cathedral pickle/food	Aqua	Molded ribbing	5
92-11-24	Body	Cathedral pickle/food	Aqua	Molded ribbing	1
92-11-795	Body	Cathedral pickle/food	Aqua	Molded ribbing	2
92-11-683	Body	Cathedral pickle/food	Aqua	Molded ribbing	1

Table 7 (continued)

92-11-630	Body	Cathedral pickle/food	Aqua	Molded ribbing	5
92-11-620	Body	Cathedral pickle/food	Aqua	Molded ribbing	5
92-11-54	Body	Cathedral pickle/food	Aqua	Molded ribbing	6
92-11-749	Body	Cathedral pickle/food	Aqua	Molded ribbing	1
92-11-744	Body	Cathedral pickle/food	Aqua	Molded dot	1
92-11-609	Body	Cathedral pickle/food	Aqua	Molded figure	1
92-11-639	Body	Cathedral pickle/food or pictorial flask	Aqua	Molded star	1
92-11-733	Body	Cathedral pickle/food	Aqua	Molded ribbing	1
92-11-185	Body	Cathedral pickle/food	Aqua	Molded ribbing	1
92-11-232	Body	Cathedral pickle/food	Aqua	Molded figure	1
92-11-635	Lip	Unknown	Aqua	None	1
92-11-341	Body	Cathedral pickle/food	Aqua	Molded ribbing	7
92-11-342	Body	Cathedral pickle/food	Aqua	Molded ribbing	1

the cap upon the nipple of the gun. The powder with which the caps are charged usually consists of fulminate of mercury mixed with half its weight of saltpeter. Half of a grain of this percussion powder constitutes the charge, which is compressed into the cap and made waterproof and air-tight by a drop of varnish.[38]

The percussion cap gun differed from the flintlock only in the firing system. Excavations at the site of the abandoned Donner party wagons in the Great Salt Lake Desert revealed percussion caps.[39] Although they found no evidence of percussion firearms at the Murphy cabin, the UNR excavators recovered six pistol-size percussion caps at the Alder Creek site (Figure 23).

Notwithstanding the popularity and availability of percussion ignition firearms in the 1840s, many people still used, and indeed preferred, the older flintlocks. John Bidwell, for example, noted that in 1841, when the Bidwell party made the first trip on the California Trail, "my gun was an old flint-lock rifle but a good one. Old hunters told me to have nothing to do with cap or percussion locks, that they were unreliable, and that if I got my caps or percussion wet I could not shoot, while if I lost my flint I could pick up another on the plains."[40] That the Donner party also carried flintlocks is quite clear from the material remains of the two mountain camps. Local residents found a flintlock gun at the Graves-Reed cabin in the nineteenth century; C. F. McGlashan dug up gunflints at the Breen cabin and the Graves-Reed cabin in 1879;[41] and the Murphy cabin excavators recovered three gunflints in 1984 (Figure 24).

It is lead balls, however, that make up the largest category of firearms-related artifacts found at the mountain camps (Figure 25). The balls vary in size from .64 caliber to birdshot, but most fall into three distinct size categories: .50–.60 caliber, .25–.35 caliber, and .10–.20 caliber. The two larger sizes probably are from Hawken or Henry rifles or cap and lock pistols; the smaller balls probably are buckshot for a shotgun. The size distributions of the lead balls from the two mountain camps are somewhat different. About half of the balls found at the Murphy cabin are less than .20 caliber, and probably are buckshot; most of the other balls are either in the .30–.40-caliber range or in the .50–.60-caliber range. In contrast, more than half of the lead balls found at Alder Creek are between .25 and .35 caliber in size; most of the others are in the buckshot size range. Perhaps the most unusual type of ammunition found at the two mountain camps is a .44-caliber conical bullet from the Murphy cabin site. The bullet is somewhat similar to that used in the Russian tigre rifle or the Norwegian breechloader of the 1850s and probably is not associated with the Donner party but may be (Figure 26).[42] In addition to the lead balls and conical bullets, the Alder Creek excavators found lead bar and sprue fragments that may have been associated with the manufacture of round lead balls.

Table 8: Glassware from the Murphy Cabin Site

Catalog No.	Element	Type	Color	Marks	Qty
P-612-209/4	Body	Unknown	Cobalt blue	None	1
P-612-101/2	Body	Bitters	Amber	None	2
P-612-125/3	Body	Unknown	Cobalt blue	None	1
P-612-280/3	Body	Medicine vial	Colorless	None	2
P-612-195/4	Body	Unknown	Cobalt blue	None	1
P-612-54/6	Body	Wine/beer	Olive green	None	3
P-612-85/1	Body/panel	Unknown	Aqua	None	1
P-612-175/1	Body	Unknown	Cobalt blue	None	1
P-612-293/3	Finish	Wine/beer	Olive green	Applied with crimped tin cap	1
P-612-311/2	Lip	Medicine vial	Colorless	None	1
P-612-293/1-1	Body	Unknown	Cobalt blue	None	1
P-612-293/1-2	Body/panel	Unknown	Aqua	None	1
P-612-171/2	Body	Unknown	Cobalt blue	None	3
P-612-158/1	Body	Unknown	Cobalt blue	None	1
P-612-103/3	Body	Unknown	Cobalt blue	None	4
P-612-6	Body	Octagonal	Cobalt blue	None	1
P-612-161/1-1	Body	Unknown	Cobalt blue	None	1
P-612-161/1-2	Rectangular flat panel or lens with decorative beveled edges	Lampshade	Amethyst	None	1

P-612-94/4	Body	Unknown	Cobalt blue	None	2
P-612-107/5-1	Body	Unknown	Cobalt blue	None	1
P-612-107/5-2	Flat lens with panel or curved decorative edge	Lampshade	Cobalt blue	None	1
P-612-155/1	Body	Cylindrical tube, 1/8" diameter	Colorless	None	1
P-612-333/3	Body	Unknown	Cobalt blue	None	1
P-612-233/6	Body	Unknown	Cobalt blue	None	2
P-612-100/8	Body	Octagonal bottle	Cobalt blue	None	6
P-612-286/2	Body	Unknown	Cobalt blue	None	1
P-612-97/3	Body	Unknown	Cobalt blue	None	1
P-612-68/2	Body	Unknown	Cobalt blue	None	1
P-612-166/3-1	Body	Bitters	Amber	None	1
P-612-173/6	Body	Unknown	Cobalt blue	None	2
P-612-166/3-2	Flat lens	Lampshade panel or decorative	Amber	None	2
P-612-284/4	Body	Unknown	Cobalt blue	None	1
P-612-86/1-1	Body	Unknown	Cobalt blue	None	3
P-612-86/1-2	Body	Unknown	Cobalt blue	None	1
P-612-194/1	Body	Unknown	Cobalt blue	None	1

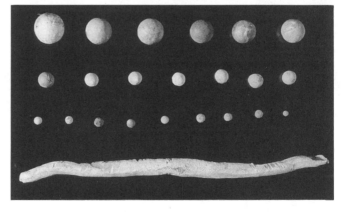

Figure 23: *(top)* Percussion caps from the Alder Creek campsite.
Figure 24: *(center)* Gunflints from the Murphy cabin site.
Figure 25: *(bottom)* Lead balls and bar from the Alder Creek campsite.

Clothing and Other Personal Gear

The excavations at the two mountain camps revealed a variety of artifacts related to clothing, adornment, or toiletries. Of these, buttons are the most numerous. C. Lynn Rogers of the University of Nevada, Reno, examined the twenty-one buttons found at the two mountain camps and reached several conclusions. Of the sixteen buttons recovered at the Murphy cabin site (Table 9), seven are stamped brass or ferrous metal "sew-throughs," which were made as early as 1835.[43] There are at least two matched sets of buttons, probably from men's trousers or work shirts. In each set, the buttons are identical in form, material, and size. This suggests that either the buttons were still attached to their garments when they were left at the site or they were intentionally removed for reuse, perhaps for patching clothing. One button is marked "Shepardson & Richards." Although it is certain that this button type was produced as early as 1835, we were unable to locate any information about the manufacturer.

Only one other button from the Murphy cabin site is datable to the Donner party period—a round gilt cuprous metal button from a man's coat or vest. The back of the button is marked "*Robinsons*Extra" (Figure 27), and there are four large seven-lobed leaves die-stamped on the front face (Figure 28). The R&W Robinson Company, which started in 1827, probably manufactured the button in Attleboro, Massachusetts, between 1836 and 1847.[44]

A few other artifact fragments found at the Murphy cabin site may be button parts but cannot be positively identified as such. Of these, two badly corroded ferrous metal disks may be parts of sew-through buttons. Two red molded or

Figure 26: Conical bullet from the Murphy cabin site.

Table 9: Buttons from the Murphy Cabin Site

Catalog No.	Material	Technique	Method of Attachment	Shape/Diameter	Decoration	Date Range
P-612-315/5A	Ferrous metal	Sanders two-piece	4-hole sew-through	Round, flat/24 lines	Japanning	1830–1930
P-612-315/5B	Ferrous metal	Stamped one-piece	4-hole sew-through	Round, flat/22 lines	Japanning	1835–1910
P-612-315/5C	Ferrous metal	Sanders two-piece	4-hole sew-through	Round, flat/20 lines	None	1830–1930
P-612-315/5D	Cuprous metal	Stamped one-piece	4-hole sew-through	Round, flat/23 lines	None	1835+
P-612-158/4	Cuprous metal	Stamped one-piece	2-hole sew-through	Round, flat/23 lines	None	1835+
P-612-100/1	Ferrous metal	Stamped one-piece	4-hole sew-through	Round, flat/22 lines	Japanning	1835+
P-612-94/6	Cuprous metal	Stamped one-piece	4-hole sew-through	Round, flat/25 lines	Shepardson & Richards	1835+
P-612-130	Cuprous metal	Stamped one-piece	Omega shank	Round, plano-convex/24 lines	Gilted and die-stamped leaf pattern *Robinsons* Extra	1836–1847
P-612-77/8	Ferrous metal	Stamped or cut one-piece	Unknown	Round, flat/25 lines	None	Unknown
P-612-149	Ferrous metal	Stamped or cut one-piece	Unknown	Round, flat/25 lines	None	Unknown

P-612-186/2-2	Dark purplish red glass	Molded or Self-shank pressed		Round/25 lines	None	1820+
P-612-80/1-1	Dark purplish red glass	Molded or Self-shank pressed		Round/25 lines	None	Unknown
P-612-167/5A,B	Cuprous metal	2 stamped one-piece studs	Two-pronged	Round, domed/23 lines	None	Unknown
P-612-213	Ferrous metal	Stamped one-piece rivet	Riveted to garment	Round/15 lines	"LS&CO-SF"	1873+
P-612-167/6	Amber plastic (lucite)	Molded	2-hole sew-through	Round, flat/19 lines	None	1935+

Figure 27: Robinson button from the Murphy cabin site, back.

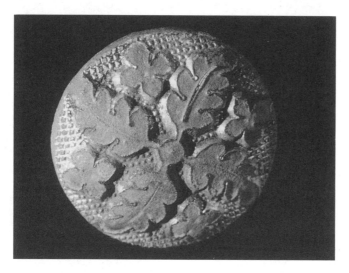

Figure 28: Robinson button from the Murphy cabin site, front.

pressed glass fragments may be fragments of buttons from a woman's outer garments or a man's vest; or they may be jewelry fragments. The fragments also include two cuprous sheet-metal studs with two prongs that may be ornaments from clothing, leather belts, or domestic animal tack but cannot be dated.

The three buttons found at the Alder Creek site (Table 10) that were produced early enough to have been left by the Donner party are all quite different from the Murphy cabin buttons. Perhaps the most unusual is a large tombac (a

Table 10: Buttons from the Alder Creek Campsite

Catalog No.	Material	Technique	Method of Attachment	Shape/ Diameter	Decoration	Date Range
92-11-561	Tombac	Cast one-piece	Cone shank	Round, concave-convex/42 lines	Polished	1700s– ca. 1820
92-11-855	Cuprous metal	Cast one-piece	Cone shank	Round, concave-plano/26 lines	None	1790– ca. 1820
92-11-81	Cuprous metal	Stamped one-piece	Omega shank	Round, concave-convex/ 28 lines	Gilt/stamped concentric rings/"... D/ooo/...GRR/ooo"[1]	1790s–
92-11-854	Cuprous and ferrous metal	Stamped three-piece rivet	Rivet to garment	Round, complex profile/19 lines	None	1875+

1. Literally stamped on button.

Figure 29: Tombac button from the Alder Creek campsite, front.

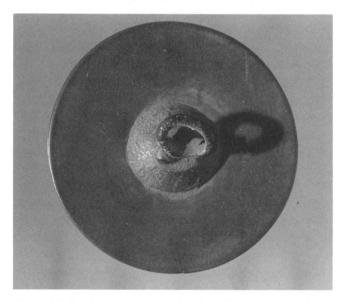

Figure 30: Tombac button from the Alder Creek campsite, back.

brasslike alloy of copper, zinc, and arsenic) button with a highly polished but undecorated face (Figures 29, 30). The button, which probably was manufactured either in the United States or Britain between the 1700s and the early 1800s, was used on men's clothing and may be from a greatcoat, coat, or vest.[45] Two other buttons, both probably manufactured in the United States or Britain between 1790 and 1820–1860, are similar in shape but smaller. One was used on a man's coat or vest, and the other was used on breeches before 1830. The Donner party period is rather late for breeches, though, or even for trousers with a fall rather than a fly opening, on which such a button might have been used.

Other archaeological evidence of clothing from the two Donner party mountain camps includes a buttonhole fragment and a shoe heel from the Murphy cabin. The editor's foreword to the 1947 reprint of McGlashan's 1880 *History of the Donner Party* includes a photograph of what is reputed to be the sole of John Denton's shoe. The heel found at the Murphy cabin site is very small, even allowing for shrinkage, and is probably from a child's shoe. Perhaps because of its small size, the heel was hand-nailed in an unusual V shaped pattern rather than around the perimeter.

BEADS

The Murphy cabin excavators found several artifacts used for personal adornment, among them beads, a pendant or earring, a brooch, and hairpins; beads are the most common (Figure 31). Lee Motz of the California Department of Parks and Recreation prepared a preliminary description and analysis of the beads in 1985;[46] Lester Ross, then of the San Bernardino County Museum, reanalyzed the beads in 1993. Tables 11–13 give detailed descriptions of the beads in the Murphy cabin assemblage. Glass beads, including two variants of drawn beads and four variants of mold-pressed types, dominate the collection, although the excavators also found a Prosser molded ceramic bead.

Several of the beads from the cabin site are unique. The ceramic bead molded by the Prosser process, which was invented in the 1830s and patented

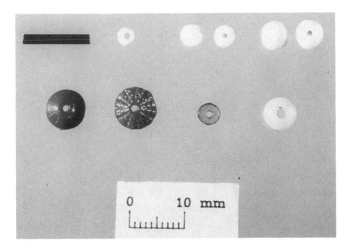

Figure 31: Beads from the Murphy cabin site.

Table 11: Drawn Glass Beads from the Murphy Cabin Site

Catalog No.	Variety	Decoration	Diaphaneity	Color	Relative Length & Shape	Size (mm)[1]	Figure No.	Kidds' No.	Qty
Monochrome bead with chopped ends ($n = 1$)									
P-612-P233/7	Ia-1	None	Opaque	Black N 0.5/	Long	1.9 x 12.4	31a	Ia2	1
Monochrome bead with a hot-tumbled finish ($n = 1$)									
P-612-152	IIa-1	None	Opaque	White N 9.25/	Short cylinder	3.3 x 1.8	31b	IIa13	1

1. Size is least diameter times length (number of sides).

Figure 32: Earring and brooch from the Murphy cabin site.

Figure 33: Hairpin and tweezers from the Murphy cabin site.

in 1840, is a very early example of the type and may be the earliest known from a well-dated archaeological context. The four mold-pressed glass beads are unreported examples of a variety being manufactured by the mid-nineteenth century. Until now, the only reported mold-pressed bead styles from this period were spherical undecorated and faceted beads with conical holes. The Murphy cabin beads with decoration and paralleled-sided holes show that the technology of mold-pressed bead manufacturing was better developed than once thought.[47]

Table 12: Mold-Pressed Beads from the Murphy Cabin Site

Catalog No.	Variety	Decoration	Diaphaneity	Color	Relative Length & Shape	Size (mm)[1]	Figure No.	Kidds' No.	Qty
					Simple monochrome beads ($n = 8$)				
P-612-89/2	MPI-1	None (mold seam forms an equatorial ridge)	Opaque	White N 9.25/	Spherical w/ narrow parallel-sided hole	Size 1	31c	—	4
P-612-9	" "					4.2 x 3.8			
P-612-94/1	" "					4.2 x 3.8			
P-612-94/1	" "					4.2 x 3.8			
						4.1 x 3.8			
P-612-106						Size 2	31d	—	3
P-612-200/3						4.9 x 5.0			
P-612-303/1						5.0 x 4.9			
						5.0 x 5.0			
P-612-11	MPI-2	None	Opaque	Red 7.5 R 4/16	Conical w/ narrow parallel-sided hole Beck's 1C2c	7.3 x 5.6	31e	—	1

Complex monochrome beads ($n = 2$)

P-612-18	MPII-1	2 impressed latitudinal circles and 12 impressed longitudinal lines forming 36 trapezoids on each end, totalling 72 trapezoids	Opaque	Red 7.5 R 3/16	Biconical w/ narrow parallel-sided hole Beck's 1C2e	7.8 x 6.6	31f	—	1
P-612-77/4	MPII-2	13 randomly ground facets	Transparent	Light purplish red 10 P 6/6 N 9.25/	Disk w/ narrow parallel-sided hole Beck's 1B1b cylinder	4.0 x 2.1	31g	—	1

1. Size is least diameter times length (number of sides).

Table 13: Prosser Molded Bead from the Murphy Cabin Site

Catalog No.	Variety	Decoration	Diaphaneity	Color	Relative Length & Shape	Size (mm)[1]	Figure No.	Kidds' No.	Qty
Simple monochrome bead ($n = 1$)									
P-612-114	PM-1	Banded	Translucent	Light greenish blue 7.5 B 7/6 N 9.25/	Spherical w/ tapered hole cylinder	6.0 x 5.1	31h	—	1

1. Size is least diameter times length (number of sides).

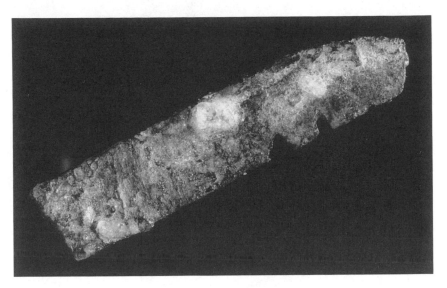

Figure 34: Pocket knife from the Murphy cabin site.

Although it is certain that the Murphy cabin beads are consistent with the Donner party period, the precise dates of their manufacture are difficult to determine. The published literature documenting the exact chronology of beads in the nineteenth-century American West is limited. Although many archaeological reports describe bead collections,[48] the archaeological context of the beads is often poorly dated, and the existing descriptions do not use comparable bead classification systems and descriptive nomenclature.

JEWELRY, HAIRPINS, AND TOILETRIES

The Murphy cabin excavators found a few artifacts other than beads that were used for, or related to, personal adornment. Jewelry found at the site includes a silver-plated dangling earring or pendant and a tin-plated brooch with a cobalt blue glass setting (Figure 32). In addition, the excavators found a hairpin and what appears to be bone tweezers at the cabin site (Figure 33).

POCKET KNIVES

Bone handle and ferrous metal blade fragments of a pocket knife or knives are among the personal artifacts found at the Murphy cabin site (Figure 34).

Tobacco Pipes

Evidence of tobacco pipes was found at the Murphy cabin site but not the Alder Creek site. Written accounts mention tobacco smoking as a personal habit of some Donner party members. Charles Stanton, for example, attempt-

Table 14: Ceramic Tobacco Pipes from the Murphy Cabin Site

Catalog No.	Element	Type	Decoration	Qty
P-612-184	Bowl	Detachable stem	Molded grooves	1 (three
P-612-224/5			and repeated	cross-mended
P-612-211/5			circles	fragments)
P-612-77/5	Unknown	White kaolin	Unknown	1
P-612-87	Bowl	White kaolin	None	1
P-612-267/2	Bowl	White kaolin	None	1
P-612-94/2	Bowl	White kaolin	"TD"	1
P-612-33A	Bowl	White kaolin	"D"	1
P-612-33B	Stem	White kaolin	"...cDougall/Glasgow"	1
P-612-193/1A	Bowl	White kaolin	"T"	1
P-612-193/1B	Stem	White kaolin	None	1
P-612-193/1C	Unknown	White kaolin	None	2

ing to escape over the mountains with the ill-fated Forlorn Hope party, was observed sitting by the campfire smoking his pipe just before he died of starvation and exposure.[49] Some women in the party smoked as well. Breen descendants, for example, remember being told that Margaret Breen was a pipe smoker.[50] Patrick Breen's diary records an instance in which tobacco contaminated the meat and caused two members of the Breen household to become ill.[51]

Most of the tobacco pipe fragments found at the Murphy cabin site are bowl and stem fragments of the so-called white kaolin clay Dublin pipes with long stems (Table 14). Four of the pipes bear the maker's mark "TD," which probably was first used either by Thomas Dennis, a pipe maker in Bristol, England, between 1734 and 1781, or by Thomas Dormer of London (Figure 35),[52] although other pipe manufacturers used the mark well into the nineteenth century as well. Another pipe fragment bears the name "McDougall Company, Glasgow, Scotland," a company that began producing pipes in 1846. In addition to these fragments the Murphy cabin site yielded a bowl from a gray detachable-stem pipe (Figure 36). It is decorated with two molded grooves and a row of repeated circles around both the bowl rim and the mouth end of the stem part.

Hand Tools

The Alder Creek excavators found several hand tools that may have been carried by the Donner party. Stylistically and technologically, however, they fall into a rather wide time bracket and could have been deposited later. The tools

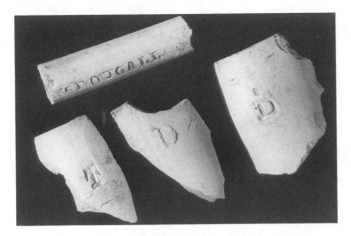

Figure 35: Clay tobacco pipes from the Murphy cabin site.

Figure 36: Decorated clay tobacco pipe bowl from the Murphy cabin site.

include spiral and other augers for a bit and brace, a masonry auger, a flat bastard file, and an iron wedge (Figure 37). Spiral augers probably were introduced into the United States in the early nineteenth century.[53]

Wagon Hardware

Several artifacts from the Alder Creek camp came from wagons, including two large iron staples (one rectangular and the other circular), an iron axle ring, a

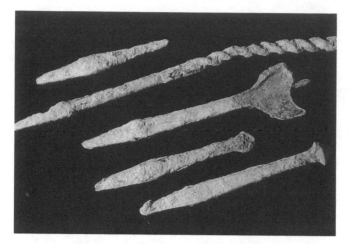

Figure 37: Hand tools from the Alder Creek campsite.

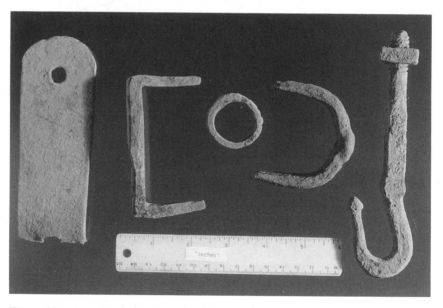

Figure 38: Wagon hardware from the Alder Creek campsite.

flat piece of strap-iron, a brass hook with a threaded end that may have been attached to a wagon box, and several wrought carriage nails with clinched ends (Figure 38). *Covered Wagon Days,* by Albert Jerome Dickson, describes the construction of a covered wagon used in the 1860s.[54] Wagon makers typically used clinchable wrought nails to fasten wagon boxes and other parts subject to shaking or other heavy vibrations. Cut nails were too brittle to be clinched until about 1840, after the invention of the Burden rotary squeezer in 1836 allowed the production of wrought iron nail plate for the first time.[55] Other artifacts from Alder Creek are parts of running gear carried by the wagons. Three links from a heavy iron chain may be the remnants of chains used for locking wagon wheels on downhill grades, essential equipment on all wagons traveling overland.[56]

Conclusions

What have we learned about the Donner party baggage from the archaeological record of the two mountain camps? Clearly, the party's baggage reflected the new economic and technological systems based on industrialism that were beginning to revolutionize America just before the Civil War. The party carried firearms, for example, that reflected the transition from flintlock to the new percussion cap technology. They brought along the most modern ceramic tableware styles of sprig-painted cups and saucers, first used by Staffordshire potters on their earthenwares in the early 1840s. They adorned themselves with ceramic beads molded by the brand-new Prosser technology, although some of the party still wore clothing fastened with old-style buttons. The baggage also reflected the social status of the Donner party members. The ceramic tableware found at the Donner family camp on Alder Creek, for example, was the cheapest decorated ware available at the time, reflecting the kind of economic decision that might be made by a middle-class family in America of the 1840s. Finally, the baggage left in the mountain camps reflected the personal beliefs of the people who carried it, the most notable example being the Roman Catholic religious medal found at the Murphy cabin site.

6 : New Directions in Donner Party Research

I n tracing the footsteps of the Donner party we have followed David Lowenthal's maxim that "memory, history, and relics offer routes to the past best traversed in combination." In many ways, of course, only the firsthand personal accounts of the participants and witnesses can testify to the Donner party's ordeal. Only these give us a glimpse of the psychological context—the personal motivations, fears, suffering, prejudices, ignorance, and stereotypes—that influenced the outcome. Whatever the "reality" of that winter in the Sierra Nevada, the experiences of the Donner party must be reconstructed ultimately from the unique life histories, mindsets, and personalities of its members.

Nevertheless, the relics left behind by the Donners and their companions provide another pathway to the past and help us establish an alternative reality—the setting within which the tragedy took place. Such a reality gives a verifiable and comparative frame of reference that is independent of the personal and subjective accounts of the participants and witnesses. The relics— artifacts, animal and plant remains, fire pits, and the like—found at the two mountain camps have taken us on an archaeological journey back to the Donner party tragedy.

The archaeological excavation of the Murphy cabin site by the University of Nevada, Reno, in 1984 yielded information about the cabin's architecture in the form of charred log and wood remnants, charcoal and ash deposits, burned bone, postholes and their remnants, and artifact distributions. As reconstructed from the evidence, the one-room cabin was twenty-five feet long, eighteen feet wide, and eight feet high with a doorway in the north wall. Artifacts related to firearms, mostly lead balls from percussion or flintlock weapons but also gunflints, dominate the artifacts found at the cabin site, although remnants of clay tobacco pipes, beads, jewelry, hairpins, buttons, glass food and medicine bottles, and ceramic tableware were also excavated. Zooarchaeological analyses showed that most of the faunal remains from the cabin site are from cattle, as would be expected, along with a horse or mule, but there were also a few surprises. Perhaps the most dramatic remains are the bear foot and caudal (tail) bones and one tooth, which accord well with written accounts recording that William Eddy, who lived in the cabin, killed a bear. Two bears, however, may be represented in the artifact collection. The accounts also say that Nicholas Clark, a member of the second relief party, killed a bear, too. Supposedly this occurred in the vicinity of the Alder Creek camp, but he may have visited the Murphy cabin afterward as well, which may explain the bear remains there.[1] Both interpretations are intriguing. Finally, the excavators found some evidence of human remains, although not of the mass grave described in firsthand accounts of General Kearny's visit to the spot on June 22, 1847, and alleged burial of the Donner party dead that he found there.

Not all of the Donner party made it as far as the lake camp. Deep snow forced the George and Jacob Donner families and their entourage to stop and camp about five miles away from the lake. C. F. McGlashan and, later, P. M. Weddell located and marked what they believed to be the site of the Donner family's camp on Alder Creek. The UNR metal detector surveys and excavation of the site in 1990 confirmed that identification, although initial excavations at the spots marked by Weddell as the Jacob Donner shelter and the George Donner shelter revealed nothing. Metal detector sweeps of the site in 1990 and on a larger scale in 1993, however, located ox shoes, horseshoes, cut nails, and a variety of other artifacts consistent with the Donner party period. The only artifact clusters were found at the meadow and anthill stump localities. Excavators at both places found a variety of artifacts dating to the Donner party period, but neither locality appears to be the site of one of the shelters. Both are probably best interpreted as places where wagons stood. The presence of burned bone fragments along with a number of domestic artifacts at the meadow locality, however, is provocative, because burned bone fragments and other food remains are typical of shelters.

Perhaps the most dramatic artifacts revealed by the Alder Creek excavation are two coins, an 1831 United States penny and an 1839 farthing minted on the Isle of Man. The possible association of the latter coin with John Denton, the only English immigrant in the Donner party, is intriguing. Other artifacts typical of the Donner party period found at the site include lead balls, percussion caps, and other firearms-related equipment; fragments of blue shell-edged plates, sprig-painted cups and bowls, and other ceramic tableware; fragments of pictorial whiskey flasks, cathedral pickle bottles, and other glass containers; hand tools; wagon hardware; and buttons. The excavators also found numerous burned bone fragments, but all are too small to identify the species.

The emigrant wagon trains traveling overland on the Oregon-California Trail carried slices of the material culture of mid-nineteenth-century America with them. In a sense, the wagons were the terrestrial equivalents of ships. They sometimes jettisoned cargo to lighten the load, and on occasion they "sank," leaving behind caches of abandoned cargo as time capsules. And also like ships, wagons often had their cargoes replenished or exchanged with traders along the way. Unlike ships, however, wagons seldom had a manifest that listed the contents of their cargo. Nevertheless, all wagon trains carried many of the same things, as detailed in contemporary guidebooks; and letters and diaries kept by the travelers often include information about what they brought with them. The wagon train carrying the Donner party was no exception. The sites of the two Donner party mountain camps are much like shipwrecks in regard to the type of archaeological information they contain. Unfortunately, much of the material originally present in these "time capsules" has been removed over the years by salvagers and relic collectors.

The UNR excavators at the two sites found numerous fragments that represent American material culture in the 1840s. The glass bottles and other containers found at the two sites—including cathedral pickle/food jars, pictorial whiskey flasks, and cobalt blue medicine or cosmetics bottles, salt dishes, or decanters—were common containers in the 1840s and, despite their fragility, obviously were used to transport food and other essentials across the country. Although known, tin cans were not commonly used to contain foodstuffs before the Civil War, and none were found at the Donner party's mountain campsites.

The clay tobacco pipes from both sites and the Roman Catholic religious medal from the Murphy cabin site provide mute testimony of the personal habits and beliefs of some members of the Donner party. Other artifacts found at the two mountain camps add to our knowledge of the clothing and adornments of the period. Some of the buttons, for example, may reflect the continuing use of older clothing styles, such as breeches or trousers with a fall rather than a fly opening. In addition, the beads found at the Murphy cabin site are rather unusual. The Prosser molded bead in the assemblage, for example, is perhaps the earliest to be found in a well-dated archaeological context; and the mold-pressed glass beads show much more stylistic diversity than expected for this early date.

Written accounts suggest that the Donner party carried both old-fashioned flintlock weapons and firearms that used the period's very latest firing system, the percussion cap. The lead balls, gunflints, and percussion caps found at the two sites reflect both technologies. Most of the other artifacts recovered at the two mountain camps are from wagons (e.g., carriage nails and wagon staples) or livestock (including ox and horse shoes, shoe nails, and harness buckles).

But the journey to the past is just beginning. Some questions about the events that took place in the high Sierra in the winter of 1846–1847 have been answered, but others remain, and new questions have been raised by the investigations. Without question, for example, the archaeological evidence confirms McGlashan and Weddell's placement of the Donner families' camp at Alder Creek. On the other hand, the excavators found no conclusive evidence of shelters, leaving as yet unanswered questions about the camp's layout and architectural details. The radioimmunoassay of bone fragments from the Murphy cabin site confirms the presence of human remains, but no direct physical evidence of cannibalism was found. The excavation also turned up no evidence of a mass burial of Donner party victims in the Murphy cabin, raising questions about the grave's location and even its existence. Could the grave be at the site of the Breen cabin or the Graves-Reed cabin? No human remains have yet been identified at the Alder Creek campsite, but no biochemical analysis of bone fragments has been done to date.

The excavation of the Murphy cabin site provided enough architectural information to reconstruct the cabin. The bone fragments recovered at the cabin site, which are mostly from cattle but also from bear and horse or mule, provided information about the foods that were available to the company and how they were processed. Both mountain campsites are repositories of artifacts representing consumer items available in 1846, and they therefore provide images of the evolution of technology. The footrings on ceramic plates from the Alder Creek site, for example, show that this manufacturing technique started earlier than previously believed.

The Demography of Disasters

Archaeology is not the only recent direction in Donner party research. Another image of the Donner party tragedy comes from the analysis of comparative life history data, statistical data on survivorship, and the biological correlates of mortality. Clearly the company typifies the common experience of groups caught on the fringe of existence. Certainly the tragedy is a story of personal endurance, heroism, conflict, weakness, and failure. But Donald Grayson of the University of Washington also points to it as wonderful "case study of mediated natural selection in action."[2] The party included people of different ages, sexes, and social groups. Death rates varied among these categories, suggesting that age and sex played a role in determining who died and who survived the ordeal. Modern studies of human mortality in extreme conditions show three important patterns: (1) the highest death rates among both males and females occur in the youngest and oldest age categories; (2) males have higher death rates than females across all age categories; and (3) males and females with larger social networks (e.g., kin groups) survive better than those without them.[3] Grayson found that the Donner party deaths generally follow this pattern.

The very young and the very old members of the party died at higher rates than those in other age categories: the death rate was much higher among children below the age of five years and adults older than forty-nine years. A notable exception to this pattern, however, is the unusually high death rate among males in the twenty–thirty-nine age group. In Appendix 1, Grayson argues that the culturally defined social roles of men and women were largely responsible for this phenomenon. The men in the Donner party, especially the young adults, were expected to perform all the heavy physical labor required along the trail. The exceptional work required of this group—clearing a trail through the heavily forested canyons of the Wasatch Range, for example—left them physically debilitated and led to their early demise in the Sierra Nevada.

Age is notoriously difficult to verify from written documents of the Donner party, of course, and this introduces some uncertainty into the conclusions drawn from the age data. Regardless of age, however, about twice as many males in the Donner party died as females, and they died much sooner, meeting another expectation from modern studies of human mortality. Explaining the difference, however, is not easy. Some studies of disasters suggest that the death rate difference between the sexes is the result of females' biological capacity to endure physiological stress from extreme cold and famine better than males.[4] Grayson notes that this may be true of the Donner party, but he also observes in Appendix 1 that the early deaths of the young adult males in the party—a substantial portion of all the male deaths—can be explained by physical exhaustion brought on by culturally defined sex role differences. If the young adult males are removed from the comparison, male and female deaths are about equal, making the argument of female biological superiority less persuasive as an explanation of Donner party survivorship. In addition, Grayson determined that the size of their social network may have played a significant role in the survivorship of young adults. The twenty- to thirty-nine-year-old survivors, of both sexes, enjoyed an average kin group size of 6.8 individuals; those who died had an average kin group size of only 2.3 individuals. Of the males in this age group, those who survived had kinship networks about twice the size of the networks of those who died. Overall, however, Grayson does not believe that differences in the size of the social network explain Donner party survivorship.

Grayson recently completed a study of survivorship in another emigrant party trapped under winter conditions similar to those endured by the Donner party.[5] In 1856, the little-known Willie handcart company, a group of Mormon immigrants from Europe, set out from Iowa City for Salt Lake City. Unable to afford animal-drawn wagons, the party of 429 men, women, and children pushed their belongings along the trail in 250-pound handcarts. After an incredible series of calamities they were caught in a snowstorm in the Rocky Mountains of Wyoming and forced to spend five weeks there. Grayson found that their pattern of survivorship was similar to that of the Donner party. Cold and starvation took sixty-eight lives, and age and sex played significant roles. The death rate of the men in the company was three times that of the women, for example, and most of those who died were older people, particularly men over forty. Grayson argues that the higher survivorship of women is biologically structured—not only by their greater body fat, smaller body size, and larger reserves of subcutaneous fat, but also by the tendency of men, because of their larger size and aggressiveness, to take greater risks and do heavier work.

Historical Climatology

Yet another image of the Donner party tragedy can be constructed from historical weather records and tree ring analyses. The accuracy of our interpretation of Donner party survivorship depends on our knowledge of the severity of the winter conditions the party members had to endure. Most accounts of the Donner party either suggest or assume that the tragedy was due, at least in part, to abnormal weather conditions during the winter of 1846–1847. *Ordeal by Hunger*, for example, bases just such a conclusion on contemporary observations of the low snowline on the western side of the Sierra Nevada.[6] The tall stumps associated with the mountain camps are often used to support the argument that there was an unusually heavy snowfall that winter.[7] The actual evidence of exceptionally harsh conditions is sparse, difficult to verify, and open to alternative interpretations. Tall stumps, for example, are also found in other parts of the Sierra Nevada, especially in the Carson Range, and are associated with winter logging in the 1860s and 1870s.

A largely untapped source of information about the winter of 1846–1847 is available in military weather records. For example, John Cordine, a retired naval officer who now lives in Reno, collects weather records from logs kept by United States Navy ships traveling off the California coast during the Mexican American War. Most interesting for our purposes are the deck logs of the sloops *Portsmouth* and *Warren*, which contain information about the weather, temperature, and barometric pressure recorded every four hours in the period from October 1846 to March 1847. Assuming that periods of observed rainfall on the California coast combined with low barometric pressure are correlated with periods of snowfall in the high Sierra, the deck logs suggest several things about the winter of 1846–1847. First, the winter appears to have been about average in the frequency and duration of snowfall. The early part of November 1846 was marked by a series of storms that correspond to the accounts of storms in Patrick Breen's diary. Other storms occurred about every two weeks from November 1846 until the beginning of February 1847, lasting about two days on average. February 1847 appears to have been largely mild and dry, and March was about the same. Tree ring studies at several places in the Sierra Nevada and other places in the Pacific Northwest and the Southwest tend to collaborate this image of the winter. Only further study of all the available evidence will resolve the contrasting images and determine the actual weather conditions of that winter of 1846–1847. All in all, however, it is clear that early fall snows played a key role in the tragedy, whatever the winter as a whole may have been like.

Conclusion

In conclusion, then, we have learned a great deal from the physical remains of the Donner party mountain camps, but there is much yet to be learned. Certainly further archaeological research at the two campsites may shed light on some of the unanswered questions raised in this book, especially those regarding the physical evidence of cannibalism, the exact locations of the shelters at the Donner family camp on Alder Creek, and the existence and location of the mass grave at the lake camp. Yet another question concerns the location of the Alder Creek camp itself. There is a remote possibility that the Donner family camp was actually closer to the main route of the California Trail, now submerged by Prosser Reservoir. Although the existing knowledge makes that unlikely, a definitive answer must await archaeological exploration of the alternative site. Only then will this nagging question be answered once and for all. The archaeological pathway to the Donner party past lies clearly in front of us.

Zooarchaeology of the Murphy Cabin Site

DONALD K. GRAYSON

Vertebrate remains from archaeological sites, in particular bones and teeth, can provide a wealth of information on the subsistence activities of the people who created the sites. It was with that thought in mind that I identified the vertebrate remains that had been excavated by Don Hardesty and his co-workers at the Murphy cabin site. Could those remains add anything to the information on food resources in the Donner mountain camps provided by the diaries and personal recollections of those who had been there? I was not the first to make this attempt. A number of years ago, Amy Dansie of the Nevada State Museum examined the same materials and composed a report that was published in 1987.[1] That report is a preliminary one, however, and does not include a complete list of the specimens identified. Without a list, it was impossible for me to know all that the collection might contain.

As it turned out, the identifiable part of the Murphy cabin faunal collection is quite small, and I could not go much beyond what Dansie had already reported. I was able to identify 141 bones and teeth from three different species: cattle (*Bos taurus*), horse or mule (*Equus* sp.), and bear (*Ursus* sp.), a species list that coincides perfectly with Dansie's. Of these fragments, only 98 can be tightly associated with the occupation of the Murphy cabin by members of the Donner party (see Table 2). Dansie identified more specimens than I did—306—but she included a large number that could be identified only as "large mammal" and which she assumed were from cattle. In addition, many of the specimens included in Dansie's report are from levels that postdate the Donner party's occupation of the site.

It is no surprise that the faunal remains relating to the Donner party's occupation of the Murphy cabin are from cattle, bear, and horse (or mule). The party brought domestic mammals with them, and it is known that William Eddy, who occupied the Murphy cabin, killed a bear in mid-November 1846.

Firsthand accounts identify that bear as a "grisly" (grizzly bear, *Ursus arctos*),[2] and Dansie identified the bear remains from the Murphy cabin as grizzly as well.[3] Species of North American bears are notoriously difficult to identify from fragmentary remains, however, and even though grizzlies are usually larger than black bears (*U. americanus*), male black bears sometimes overlap female grizzlies in size.[4]

The single bear tooth in the Murphy cabin collection, the crown of a lower second molar, is 2.52 centimeters long (Dansie reported two bear teeth; I found only one). For reference, in a collection of twelve modern black bears from Illinois, Graham found the length of this tooth to range from 1.76 to 2.26 centimeters,[5] suggesting that the Murphy cabin specimen may indeed be from a grizzly bear.

In fact, two bears may be represented in this collection. As Dansie also observed, the most common bear bones in the collection are from the feet: of the fourteen bear specimens that can be securely assigned to the Donner party occupation, eleven are foot bones, either phalanges or metapodials, two are caudal bones, and one is a tooth. Although it is not possible from the size or the form of the foot bones to tell what kind of bear they are from, a female grizzly bear in the collections of the Illinois State Museum (specimen 690738) with a lower second molar comparable in size to the one from the Murphy cabin (2.54 cm) has phalanges much larger than the Murphy cabin specimens. For instance, the Murphy cabin collection has two measurable first phalanges. On these, the distal condyles at the midpoint of the palmar surface are 0.83 and 0.93 centimeter wide. The smallest first phalanx from the Illinois State Museum specimen measured 1.00 centimeter at this point. Likewise, there are two measurable second phalanges. The maximum width at the midpoint of the distal end of the distal articular surface of these is 0.93 and 1.05 centimeters. In the Illinois State Museum specimen, the smallest second phalanx measured 1.02 centimeters at this point. These numbers suggest that two individuals may be represented in the Murphy cabin collection. Without measuring a much larger sample of modern grizzly and black bear bones and teeth, however, it is not possible to know.

In addition to the eleven bear foot bones, there are two fragmentary caudal (tail) vertebrae of bear in the faunal assemblage. Twelve of these thirteen bone fragments are clearly burned. The tooth has not been burned; in fact, it looks remarkably fresh given the context from which it came. That the bones were burned while the tooth was not might also suggest that two different individuals are represented in the assemblage. Of course, it might also simply reflect the fact that different body parts were treated differently by the human occupants of the site.

Given that Eddy shot the bear and that the Eddy family occupied the Murphy cabin, it is interesting that nearly all the bear bones discovered at this site are from an area of the bear that is of relatively low nutritional value—the paws. There are other ways to interpret this information, however. It is quite possible that other parts of the skeleton were so intensely utilized that they are no longer identifiable, or that by the time professional excavations were conducted at the site the other bones had already been removed or had decayed beyond recognition.

Three bones in the collection show clear indications of having been cut with metal tools. a tibia shaft and two rib shafts; a fourth specimen, a metatarsal shaft, may also have been cut with a metal tool. Dansie's report mentions the tibia as the largest and best preserved ox bone in the collection.[6] Now that the stratigraphy at the Murphy cabin is better understood, we know that this specimen actually came from feature 8 (see Figure 7). Unless some disturbance moved it upward, it was deposited after the Donner party had abandoned the cabin. The other cut specimens, however, are securely associated with the Donner party's occupation.

Not much that is new or conclusive can be said based on ninety-eight identified bones. The collection does confirm what we know from the written accounts: that the occupants of the Murphy cabin made extensive use of their domestic cattle, and also that they had access to a bear. There is documentary evidence to suggest that two bears might be represented in the collection, but proving that would require measuring the teeth and phalanges of a large series of modern bears to determine whether a tooth as large as the Murphy cabin specimen could have come from an animal with phalanges as small as those represented in the collection.

APPENDIX 2

Ceramics from the Alder Creek Camp

GEORGE L. MILLER

The assemblage comprises items broken or abandoned by the Donner party in their winter camp of 1846–1847, and is thus a case of the site dating the ceramics rather than vice versa. Unfortunately, the sherds from the Alder Creek camp are very small (the vast majority would fit on a dime with room to spare) and badly frost pitted, which makes it difficult to produce a minimal vessel count. Further, the site appears to have been rather thoroughly worked over by relic and souvenir hunters. Given these limitations, the amount of information that can be gleaned from the collection is quite small. This is truly unfortunate because archaeologists rarely have an opportunity to look at collections from such a tightly dated site.

None of the sherds appears to postdate the Donner occupation, and all of the types present appear to be styles that were introduced in the mid-1830s or early 1840s. This suggests that the collection was assembled in one of two possible ways: either the households that owned them were set up after about 1835, or the travelers purchased new ceramics on setting out for California. All of the ceramics found are of the cheapest types with painted decoration that were available at the time; none of the sherds appears to be from plain (undecorated) creamware, which would have been the cheapest tableware available, or from "dipped" ware, which would have been the cheapest decorated tableware.

Plates

All of the plate sherds with decoration are from unscalloped blue shell-edged plates. Those with enough of the decorated surface present to allow classification show simple shallow molded repetitive patterns. There may be two entire plates present, but it is difficult to be sure because such a small part of the decorative surface has survived. This type of shell edge made its appearance in the 1840s and continued to be manufactured through the 1850s.[1]

Cups and Saucers

The cups and saucers with decoration are all of a type known as sprig painted; that is, they have small floral designs with a lot of open white space in between the flower sprigs. Advertisements for sprig-painted porcelain tea, table, and toilet wares were published as early as 1831. The *National Daily Intelligencer* advertised sprig-painted porcelain wares in ads such as the following, dating from 1831 to 1835.[2]

> October 17, 1831   P. Mauro and Sons, Auctioneers
> 2 sets unhandled Tea China, green sprig
> 6 sets unhandled Tea China, pink sprig
>
> October 15, 1835   F. A. Ellery
> Plain White French China Dinner ware, in sets
> Plain Green Sprig Dinner ware, in sets
> Gold band Dinner ware, in sets
>
> Plain white, White and Gold, and Sprig China Coffees
> and Saucers, Cups and Saucers, Plates and Bowls,
> Tea Pots, Sugars, Creams, and Cup Plates
>
> China Tea Sets, white and gold, plain white, rich
> flowered, and sprig patterns
>
> China Toilet Sets, white and gold, plain white, rich
> flowered, and sprig patterns

Obviously, there is a strong correlation between sprig painting and French porcelain. The Staffordshire potters seem to have taken up sprig painting on their earthenwares in the early 1840s.

The colors used in painting the sprigged earthenware in this collection are important for dating the sherds. A group of new chrome colors, including red, black, and apple green, began to be used on Staffordshire earthenwares in the early 1830s.[3] In the 1830s these colors were used for larger painted floral patterns. One of the hallmarks of the change is the use of black stems for the plants, as opposed to the blue or brown stems generally found on earlier polychrome painted wares.

Most likely the sprig-painted cups, saucers, and bowls found at the Alder Creek site were purchased in the early 1840s, or possibly just before the trip west. As mentioned above, the assemblage comprises the cheapest tea and table ware with painted decoration available, and none of the sherds is from plain undecorated creamware, which would have been the cheapest ceramic tableware available. One surprising thing about the assemblage is the absence of dipt ("dipped") wares, which would have been the cheapest types of bowls available with any kind of decoration, although this may simply reflect the small size of the collection.

Footring Sherds

The several footring sherds from plates suggest a date in the 1840s or later. These footring sherds have wide and flat free-standing footrings, a style that came into use during the 1840s and became one of the most common types from then until around the late 1880s. I had always associated these footrings with plates produced on a jigger (an automatic plate-throwing machine), but this type of footring appears to be just a change in style rather than the result of a new technology. The known date of the Alder Creek site helps to shed some light on this issue because the jigger was not introduced into the Staffordshire potteries until 1844 and was withdrawn shortly thereafter.[4] It was reintroduced in 1847, again in just a few potteries.[5] Given that these footrings were recovered from the Alder Creek camp, and thus must have been purchased before 1846, it is extremely unlikely that the vessels were jigger thrown. Therefore, the broad, flat footrings are simply a different style rather than the product of a new technological process.

Pearlware versus Whiteware

There is a slight bluish tint to the glaze of the shell-edged plates in the assemblage, which brings up the question of whether or not they are pearlware. To put the question into context, it is necessary to review the development of pearlware and how it is defined by archaeologists. According to the simplest definition, pearlware is any glazed white earthenware whose glaze shows blue tinting; unfortunately, that is the definition on which archaeologists have settled. As a result, there are "pearlware" vessels dating from circa 1775 to circa 1845.

The definition breaks down, however, because pearlware continued to evolve in the nineteenth century and was not of great importance to potters. Potters generally classified wares by decoration, such as "CC," "painted," "dipt," "edged," or "printed," and seldom used the term *pearlware* at all. Furthermore, the Wedgwood factory used at least six different formulas for pearlware; for example, what potters marked "pearl" in the 1860s is what archaeologists today would call whiteware.[6]

Even the term *pearlware* is a problem. It evolved from Josiah Wedgwood's new 1779 glaze, "Pearl White," which was just his version of what other potters had been producing since at least 1775 and calling "China Glaze."[7] Perhaps the best solution to the problem of classification would be to consider the visual effect the potters intended to create. The Staffordshire potters introduced blue into the glaze in an attempt to make an earthenware that would replace Chinese porcelain. The new glaze was needed for several reasons. First was the increased market demand for a substitute. The British East India Company stopped importing Chinese porcelain in 1791, and Champion's patent, which was renewed in 1775, prevented English potters from manufacturing hard paste porcelain and simply duplicating the Chinese wares.[8] Second, technological developments made the new earthenware possible. Cornish clays were introduced in the potteries in 1775, and a cobalt refining furnace was set up in Staffordshire in 1772. Out of this social and technological context, in about 1775, evolved what the Staffordshire potters called "China Glaze."[9] The glaze of the new ware was tinted blue to make it look like Chinese porcelain. Chinese shapes such as the handleless tea bowl were copied, along with Chinese-style patterns with blue as the dominant color. The newer ware has a very distinct blue tint that is easily visible on undecorated surfaces, and not just in places where the glaze has puddled, such as around footrings.

The issue is confused by the use of cobalt in wares that appeared on the American market after the War of 1812. Cobalt blue is still present in the glaze; however, it was used to cancel the yellow tint in the lead glaze. The overall impression one gets when viewing the undecorated surfaces of these wares is that they are white, not blue tinted. In other words, if one can see only the blue tinting where the glaze is puddled, then one is looking at a whiteware. On that basis, I would say that the sherds from the Alder Creek camp are whiteware.

The Timing of Donner Party Deaths

DONALD K. GRAYSON

In an earlier paper on the demographics of Donner party deaths, I observed that three factors mediated who lived and who died.[1] Death struck preferentially at males, at the oldest and youngest members of the party, and at those traveling alone or with small kin groups. In reaching those conclusions, I looked briefly at the order in which the deaths occurred, but I relied primarily on comparing those who survived with those who did not. In this appendix I take a more detailed look at the timing of the deaths of Donner party members after they reached the Sierran encampment and apply principles of human biology to explain the order of the deaths.

It is well known that the males of most species of mammals are more aggressive than the females, their larger body size and greater physical strength being just two of the many traits associated with that more aggressive nature.[2] Our own species is no exception to this general rule; the differences in male and female body size and physical strength are quite obvious. It is thus no surprise to learn that among "white" Americans between the ages of twenty-five and twenty-nine years, the average female body weight is 78 percent of the average male body weight;[3] nor is it surprising that American and European women have only 55–65 percent of the isometric body strength of men.[4] The greater aggressiveness of human males in social contexts is equally visible and accounts for the fact that males commit far more violent crimes than females do.

In 1990, for instance, 88.7 percent of the violent crimes committed in the United States were committed by men.[5] Indeed, cross-cultural studies show that even though levels of aggression in males vary significantly from one society to the next, within particular societies young boys are routinely more aggressive than young girls.[6]

In Western society, males routinely perform a number of tasks for which they are better fitted than females by virtue of their larger body size and more aggressive nature. For example, while women constituted 44 percent of the U.S. civilian labor force in 1988, only 3.8 percent of the loggers in that force were women.[7] And it is no surprise that when the Donner party hacked a trail through the Wasatch Range during August 1846, it was the men, not the women, who bore the brunt of the labor.[8]

There is no way to know exactly how much this grueling labor affected the strength of the Donner party men, but they surely emerged from the Wasatch Range with their internal energy stores drained, stores they were unable to renew during the long and arduous trip across the Great Basin Desert that followed. After the party was ensnared by the Sierran snows in November, the men were again charged with conducting the most difficult chores.[9] Given these facts, the mortality records should show that the men died sooner than the women after the company was trapped by the Sierran snows, and that the difference in the timing of their deaths was substantial.

The Chronology of Donner Party Deaths

Table 15 provides demographic information about the Donner party members who died after entrapment, including age, sex, the size of the family group with which each traveled, and the date of death. The final column in this table measures the number of days that elapsed between the first day of encampment and death, a number I refer to as "days-to-death." The first death occurred on December 15; the last one came 108 days later, on April 1.

The dates of death shown in the table are primarily from two sources: Patrick Breen's diary and George R. Stewart's *Ordeal by Hunger*.[10] Not all of the dates of death were recorded by diarists, and it was necessary for me to estimate some of them. I did this by establishing the interval between the last date when that person was mentioned as being alive and the first mention that he or she had succumbed, and used the midpoint of this interval as the date of death. For instance, firsthand accounts establish that young James Eddy was alive on March 3, 1847, but had died by March 13. As a result, I estimated his date of death as March 8. All the estimated dates appear in italics in Table 15.

In my earlier paper I observed that the males of the Donner party died both at a greater rate than the females and sooner than the females. Table 15 makes this fact evident. The first death among the stranded party occurred on Decem-

Table 15: Donner Party Members Who Died after Reaching the Sierra Nevada

Name	Sex	Age	Family Size	Date of Death	Days-to-Death
Donner, Jacob	Male	65	16	December 15	1
Williams, Baylis	Male	24	2	December 15	1
Reinhardt, Joseph	Male	30	1	*December 15*	1
Shoemaker, Samuel	Male	25	1	*December 15*	1
Smith, James	Male	25	1	*December 15*	1
Stanton, Charles	Male	35	1	December 21	7
Antonio	Male	23	1	December 24	10
Graves, Franklin	Male	57	12	December 24	10
Dolan, Patrick	Male	40	1	December 25	11
Murphy, Lemuel	Male	12	13	December 26	12
Burger, Charles	Male	30	1	December 29	15
Fosdick, Jay	Male	23	12	January 5	22
Keseberg, Lewis Jr.	Male	1	4	January 24	41
Murphy, John	Male	15	13	January 30	47
McCutchen, Harriet	Female	1	3	February 2	50
Eddy, Margaret	Female	1	4	February 4	52
Eddy, Eleanor	Female	25	4	February 7	55
Spitzer, Augustus	Male	30	1	February 8	56
Elliott, Milton	Male	28	1	February 9	57
Pike, Catherine	Female	1	13	February 20	68
Denton, John	Male	28	1	February 24	72
Keseberg, Ada	Female	3	4	February 24	72
Hook, William	Male	12	16	February 28	76
Donner, Lewis	Male	3	16	March 7	83
Donner, Isaac	Male	5	16	March 8	84
Graves, Elizabeth Cooper	Female	47	12	March 8	84
Graves, Franklin Jr.	Male	5	12	March 8	84
Eddy, James	Male	3	4	*March 8*	84
Foster, George	Male	4	13	*March 8*	84
Donner, Elizabeth	Female	45	16	*March 11*	87
Murphy, Lavina	Female	50	13	*March 19*	95
Donner, Samuel	Male	4	16	*March 20*	96
Donner, George	Male	62	16	*March 26*	102
Donner, Tamsen	Female	45	16	*March 27*	103
Graves, Elizabeth	Female	1	12	*April 1*	108

Note: Estimated dates of death are in italics.

ber 15; by the end of January, fourteen males—but not a single female—had died. From February to April, deaths were evenly distributed by sex: ten females and an additional eleven males lost their lives. A great deal more can be learned from the numbers than this, however.

Death Takes a Holiday

Figure 39 displays the deaths that occurred over the 108 days of the winter encampment. The deaths are grouped by five-day intervals beginning with December 15, the date of the first death (as a result of this grouping procedure, the death of the first female, Harriet McCutchen, is shown as contemporaneous with that of John Landrum Murphy, even though Murphy died first). Two aspects of this figure deserve special mention. First, as I have already observed, many males died before females began to die. Second, there was a period of eighteen days, from January 6 through January 23, when no member of the Donner party died. When the deaths resumed, both sexes died, and in almost equal numbers.

The males who succumbed in the first wave of death not only died before any females died, but once they began to die, many were lost in a short time. Of the fourteen males who succumbed before the first female death, eleven died during the fifteen-day interval that began on December 15 and ended on December 29. Over the next thirty-three days, only three more males died (see Table 15). Why did so many males succumb so quickly, and why was there an eighteen-day lull in deaths?

Figure 40 displays the relationship between age and days-to-death for all those who died after reaching the mountain camps. Figure 41 shows this relationship for males alone and suggests that days-to-death is inversely related to age: the youngest survived longest, and, with one exception, the oldest died first. Statistically, this relationship is weak (Spearman's rho, $r_s = -0.489$), but significant ($p = .013$).[11]

The exception is sixty-two-year-old George Donner. In October, as the Donners were struggling into the Sierra Nevada, Donner cut his hand badly while repairing a broken axle. The wound soon became infected and never healed. Once the Donner camp was established, he could neither attempt to escape nor fend for himself. His wife, Tamsen, was given the opportunity to leave with rescuers from the Sacramento Valley, but refused in order to remain with her husband. With her care, Donner survived until about March 26. Tamsen survived only a day longer.[12]

As a result of his injury, George Donner was just as dependent as any child in the stranded party, and this dependency probably allowed him to survive as long as he did. Indeed, statistical analysis shows him to be an outlier 2.7 stan-

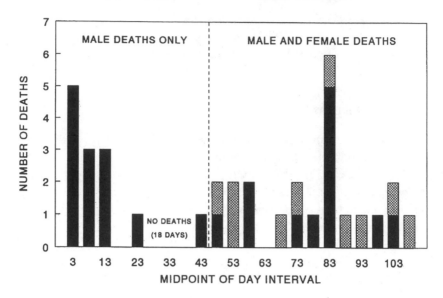

Figure 39: Deaths within the Sierran encampment of the Donner party. The first death occurred on December 15, 1846; the last occurred 108 days later on April 1, 1847. The midpoint of day interval is the midpoint of the interval between the time when documents last mention that the person was alive and the time when documents first mention that he or she had died.

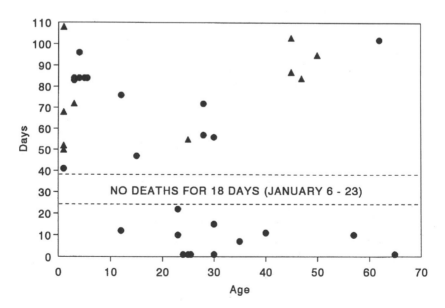

Figure 40: The relationship between age and days-to-death among the Donner party members who reached the Sierra Nevada. The first death occurred on December 15, 1846; the last occurred 108 days later on April 1, 1847. Closed circles = males; triangles = females.

dard deviations from the mean in the relationship depicted in Figure 41.[13] Without Tamsen to care for him, George Donner would likely have died far earlier. Without him, the correlation between age and days-to-death, r_s, is -0.666 ($p < .001$).

It is nevertheless clear that age played a major role in determining the order of deaths among the males of the Donner party, with older males dying before younger ones. But this relationship by itself does not account for the rapidity with which death struck prime-of-life males between the ages of 20 and 40. Of the twelve men of this age who died in the mountain camps, nine died between December 15 and January 5. The twelve males lost before the eighteen-day lull in deaths averaged 32.4 years of age; the other thirteen males who died averaged only 15.4 years.

While the deaths of Jacob Donner (age 65) and Franklin Graves (age 57) can be attributed to their advanced years, the deaths of the men between the ages of 20 and 40 cannot. I have argued that these deaths were in part a result of the fact that the men involved did not travel in large family groups.[14] Seven of them were not traveling with any family members. The males who died before the eighteen-day lull in deaths were part of family groups that averaged 5.2 individuals in size, whereas those who died after the lull traveled with families that averaged 9.9 members. As a whole, the chronology of deaths among

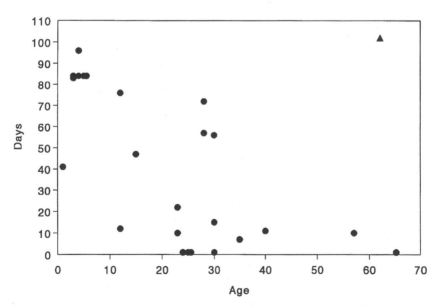

Figure 41: The relationship between age and days-to-death among the Donner party males who reached the Sierra Nevada. The first death occurred on December 15, 1846; the last occurred on March 26, 1847. Triangle = George Donner.

the Donner party males is positively correlated with family size, though that correlation is not impressive ($r_s = 0.531, p = .006$).

These facts alone, however, cannot account for the speed with which the prime-age males died. Certainly another factor relating to their quick deaths is the fact that these men had depleted their energy reserves crossing the Wasatch Range four months earlier and had been unable to rebuild them. Lacking those reserves, prime-age males were the first to succumb under the harsh conditions of the initial weeks of the forced encampment. Death then took a holiday until the conditions in the Sierra Nevada began to take a toll on those who had been in better physical condition at the onset of the ordeal. It appears that it took eighteen days for this to happen. In fact, exhaustion helps to explain why age and days-to-death are inversely related among the Donner party males who died: the males who exhausted themselves, and thus died quickly, were, as I noted, an average of seventeen years older than the males who died after the lull in deaths. The male children had not exhausted themselves in transit: it was the men who had done that.

In short, there were two separate episodes of death among the members of the Donner party who reached the Sierra Nevada. The first episode involved prime-age males who had exhausted their energy reserves earlier in the trip; the second episode struck both males and females. Given that males excel at, and were expected to perform, the kinds of short-term labor-intensive tasks that were needed to escape the Wasatch Range and to promote the company's survival in the winter camps, all this is simply another way of saying that the men who died almost immediately were doomed by their sex and age.

The quick deaths of the prime-age adult men left the survivors largely devoid of those who normally would have hunted for food and cut wood for fuel. Without a full complement of young males to accomplish those tasks, the Donner party members became far more dependent on rescuers than they would otherwise have been.

Death among the Females

After the lull in deaths, the sequence in which males died tended to be weakly mediated by family size ($r_s = 0.511, p = .09$), but not by age ($r_s = -0.344, p > .20$; George Donner excluded). The relationship between age and days-to-death among the ten female members of the Donner party who died is quite different from that shown by the males (Figure 42). For the ten females as a group, the relationship between age and days-to-death is not significant ($r_s = 0.464, p = .18$). However, the group includes one infant, Elizabeth Graves, who died in the Sacramento Valley after having been rescued. If she is removed from the analysis, the relationship between age and days-to-death for the female members of the Donner party is quite significant($r_s = 0.817, p = .007$).

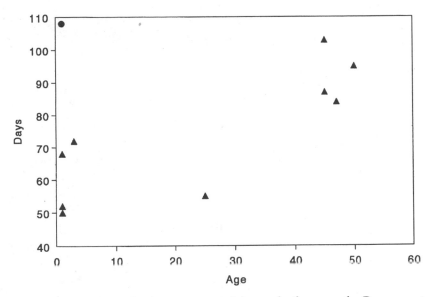

Figure 42: The relationship between age and days-to-death among the Donner party females who reached the Sierra Nevada. The first death occurred on February 2, 1847; the last occurred on April 1, 1847. Closed circle = Elizabeth Graves.

Unlike the corresponding relationship for the males who died, this relationship is positive: older females survived longer than younger females before dying. The reason for the different age-death relationship among adult males, again, is that they arrived in the Sierra Nevada in far poorer condition than the adult females.

I noted above that the relationship between family size and days-to-death is weak among the Donner party males. The corresponding relationship for Donner party females, however, is quite strong ($r_s = 0.724, p = .018$; without Elizabeth Graves, $r_s = 0.855, p = .003$). While speed of death among the males was mediated to some extent by age and family size, family size played a far more significant role among the females. This difference is likely the result of the fact that the beneficial effects of being surrounded by family members were overridden in males by the loss of energy associated with the strenuous tasks they were expected to, and did, perform. That is, the benefits gained by the Donner party men by belonging to larger family groups tended to be lost by virtue of their sex.

Conclusions

A comparison of the Donner party members who lived with those who died suggests that sex, age, and family group size played the major role in mediating survivorship in the group.[15] The chronology of the Donner party deaths in the Sierra Nevada suggests that those variables were at work here. Among the males, prime-age men died with remarkable speed, apparently because their energy reserves had been depleted. Males traveling alone or with small family groups died sooner than those who traveled with larger families. No females died until after fourteen males had already lost their lives. Once the females began to die, the children went first and the women later; and, more so than with the males, family group size and longevity were positively correlated in females. That family size played a larger role in increasing longevity among the females than among the males is likely due to the tremendous energy losses that the men suffered as a result of "acting like men."

Many other questions can be asked about the pattern of death among the Donner party members. For instance, did the expected lifespan of an individual in the Sierra Nevada decrease when that person stayed behind when other family members were rescued? Did it decrease as other family members died, as the case of Tamsen Donner certainly seems to suggest? While such issues remain to be explored, it is clear that although the pattern of deaths within the Donner party is complex, it can be readily explained by the biology of males and females. Although what happened to the Donner party was tragic, the deaths at the two winter camps can teach us much about how men and women respond to extreme conditions.

Acknowledgments

My thanks to Eric A. Smith, Donald L. Hardesty, and David B. Madsen for comments on an earlier version of this appendix.

NOTES

Introduction

1. The *California Star,* May 22, 1847, was the first to publish Breen's diary. A more complete version is printed in George R. Stewart, *Ordeal by Hunger* (Boston: Houghton Mifflin, 1936; rev. ed., Lincoln: University of Nebraska Press, 1960), 257–67.

2. Reed's diary is printed in Stewart, *Ordeal by Hunger,* 271–76.

3. Virginia Reed Murphy, "Across the Plains in the Donner Party," *Century Illustrated Magazine* (July 1891); Eliza P. Donner Houghton, *The Expedition of the Donner Party and Its Tragic Fate* (Chicago: A. C. McClurg, 1911).

4. Bryant, *What I Saw in California* (Philadelphia: D. Appleton, 1848).

5. Thornton, *Oregon and California in 1848* (New York: Harper and Brothers, 1849).

6. McGlashan, *The History of the Donner Party* (Truckee, Calif.: Crowley and McGlashan, 1879).

7. King, *Winter of Entrapment* (Toronto: P. D. Meany, 1992; rev. ed., Lafayette, Calif.: K&K Publications, 1994).

8. Bernard DeVoto, *Year of Decision, 1846* (Boston: Houghton Mifflin, 1943); Dale L. Morgan, ed., *Overland in 1846: Diaries and Letters of the California-Oregon Trail,* 2 vols. (Georgetown, Calif.: Talisman Press, 1963); Kristin Johnson, *"Unfortunate Emigrants": Narratives of the Donner Party* (Logan: Utah State University Press, 1996).

9. Francis C. Robinson, *The Donner Party in Fiction,* University of Colorado Studies, Series in Language and Literature 10, (Boulder: University of Colorado, 1966), 87–93.

10. Hoffman Birney, *Grim Journey* (New York: Minton, Balch and Company, 1934).

11. See King, *Winter of Entrapment,* 143–64, for an extended discussion. Also see Vardis Fisher's *The Mothers: An American Saga of Courage* (New York: Vanguard Press, 1943), Julia Cooley Altrocchi's *Snow-Covered Wagons, a Pioneer Epic* (New York: Macmillan, 1936), Ruth Whitman's *A Woman's Journey* (Cambridge, Mass.: Alice James Books, 1985), and Jeanette Gould Maino's *Left Hand Turn: A Story of the Donner Party Women* (Modesto, Calif.: privately printed, 1987).

12. David Lowenthal, *The Past Is a Foreign Country* (Cambridge: Cambridge University Press, 1985).

13. Ibid., 249.

14. Mark Leone and Parker Potter, Introduction to *The Recovery of Meaning: Historical Archaeology in the Eastern United States*, ed. Mark Leone and Parker Potter, 1–22 (Washington, D.C.: Smithsonian Institution Press, 1987).

15. Geoffrey Bibby, *The Testimony of the Spade* (New York: A. A. Knopf, 1956).

16. McGlashan, *History of the Donner Party*, 258.

17. Ibid., 259–60.

18. Ibid., 258–59.

19. Stewart, *Ordeal by Hunger*, 304.

20. Jack Steed, *The Donner Party Rescue Site, Johnson's Ranch on Bear River*, rev. and exp. ed. (Sacramento: privately published, 1993), 76–77.

21. Ibid., 77–82.

22. Bruce Hawkins and David Madsen, *Excavation of the Donner-Reed Wagons* (Salt Lake City: University of Utah Press, 1990).

23. Ibid., 131–32.

24. Donald L. Hardesty, "Archaeology of the Donner Party Tragedy," *Nevada Historical Society Quarterly* 30 (Winter 1987): 246–68.

25. McGlashan, *History of the Donner Party*, 260.

26. C. F. McGlashan, Letter to the Native Sons of the Golden West, in *From the Desk of Truckee's C. F. McGlashan*, ed. M. Nona McGlashan and Betty H. McGlashan (Truckee, Calif.: Truckee-Donner Historical Society, n.d.), 117.

27. Ibid., 111.

28. Donald L. Hardesty, "Donner Party Archaeology," *Overland Journal* 10, no. 3 (1992): 18–26; Donald L. Hardesty and Susan Lindström, "Archaeology of the Donner Family Camp" (Report prepared for the Tahoe National Forest, Nevada City, Calif., 1990).

1 : The Donner Party Saga

1. John Unruh, *The Plains Across* (Urbana: University of Illinois Press, 1979); Richard White, *"It's Your Misfortune and None of My Own": A New History of the American West* (Norman: University of Oklahoma Press, 1991), 189.

2. George Stewart, *Ordeal by Hunger* (Lincoln: University of Nebraska Press, 1960); Joseph King, *Winter of Entrapment*, rev. ed.; Richard Lingenfelter, *Death Valley and the Amargosa* (Berkeley: University of California Press, 1986), 40–47; White, *It's Your Misfortune and None of My Own*, 202.

3. Unruh, *The Plains Across*, 110.

4. Dale L. Morgan, *The Humboldt* (New York: Farrar and Rinehart, 1943), 115–21.

5. Quoted in Stewart, *Ordeal by Hunger*, 283–84.

6. Joseph A. King (personal communication) has evidence that Luis and Salvador were Plains Miwok Cosumne with the names Eema Ochej and Queyuen, respectively.

7. Sarah Winnemucca Hopkins, *Life among the Piutes* (Boston: privately printed, 1883; reprint, Reno: University of Nevada Press, 1994), 12–13.

8. Joseph A. King and Jack Steed, "John Baptiste Trudeaux of the Donner Party: Rascal or Hero?" *California History* 74, no. 2 (1995): 171–72.

9. Stewart, *Ordeal by Hunger*, 257.

10. Ibid., 262.

2 : The Donner Party and Overland Emigration, 1840–1860

1. See Unruh, *The Plains Across*; and John Mack Faragher, *Women and Men on the Overland Trail* (New Haven: Yale University Press, 1979); see also Merrill J. Mattes, *The Great Platte River Road* (Lincoln: Nebraska State Historical Society, 1969).

2. Unruh, *The Plains Across*, 119.

3. Eliza P. Donner Houghton, *The Expedition of the Donner Party and Its Tragic Fate* (Chicago: A. C. McClurg, 1911), 3–4.

4. Unruh, *The Plains Across*, 90–94.

5. Dale E. Morgan, ed., *Overland in 1846: Dairies and Letters of the California Trail*, 2 vols. (Georgetown, Calif.: Talisman Press, 1963), 2:491.

6. Bryant, *What I Saw in California* (Palo Alto: Lewis Osborne, 1967), 37; Morgan, *Overland in 1846*, 1:249; Stewart, *Ordeal by Hunger*, 17.

7. Thornton, *Oregon and California in 1848*, 13, 25–26.

8. Quoted in Morgan, *Overland in 1846*, 2:531.

9. Houghton, *Expedition of the Donner Party*, 4.

10. Morgan, *Overland in 1846*, 1:307.

11. Quoted in Stewart, *Ordeal by Hunger*, 18.

12. Quoted in Morgan, *Overland in 1846*, 2:491.

13. Quoted in McGlashan, *History of the Donner Party*, 25.

14. Faragher, *Women and Men on the Overland Trail*, 192–93.

15. Morgan, *Overland in 1846*, 2:526–27, 555, 562; Stewart, *Ordeal by Hunger*, 132; McGlashan, *History of the Donner Party*, 49–50, 71, 91, 175, 178, 184, 207, 210.

16. Houghton, *Expedition of the Donner Party*, 10.

17. McGlashan, *History of the Donner Party*, 17, 21; Unruh, *The Plains Across*, 97–100; Faragher, *Women and Men on the Overland Trail*, 24–25.

18. Unruh, *The Plains Across*, 252; Louise Barry, *Beginning of the West: Annals of the Kansas Gateway to the American West, 1540–1854* (Topeka: Kansas State Historical Society, 1972), 583–84.

19. Houghton, *Expedition of the Donner Party*, 17; Thornton, *Oregon and California in 1848*, 46.

20. Barry, *Beginning of the West*, 584–85.

21. Unruh, *The Plains Across*, 122–24.

22. McGlashan, *History of the Donner Party*, 21; Morgan, *Overland in 1846*, 2:591–92.

23. Quoted in Morgan, *Overland in 1846*, 2:563.

24. Morgan, *Overland in 1846*, 2:563, 582.

25. Quoted in ibid., 617.

26. Unruh, *The Plains Across*, 124, 126.

27. Houghton, *Expedition of the Donner Party*, 22; Thornton, *Oregon and California in 1848*, 60–61; Morgan, *Overland in 1846*, 1:278–79; 2:579, 611, 614–15.

Stanton sent a letter to his brother from Bear River via Fort Bridger, but it is not known whether it was carried to the latter place by an Indian, a mountain man, or returning emigrants. See Morgan, *Overland in 1846*, 2:762.

28. Unruh, *The Plains Across*, 130–35; Houghton, *Expedition of the Donner Party*, 22–23; Stewart, *Ordeal by Hunger*, 23, 33–34.

29. Unruh, *The Plains Across*, chap. 5; Murphy, "Across the Plains," 3–4; Morgan, *Overland in 1846*, 2:561–62, 583–84; Houghton, *Expedition of the Donner Party*, 14–15, 21–22, 28–29.

30. Unruh, *The Plains Across*, 185.

31. Stewart, *Ordeal by Hunger*, 240.

32. Gary Topping, "Overland Emigrants, the California Trail, and the Hastings Cut-off," in *Excavation of the Donner-Reed Wagons*, Bruce Hawkins and David Madsen, 11–15 (Salt Lake City: University of Utah Press, 1990); Thomas H. Hunt, *Ghost Trails to California* (New York: Weathervane Books, 1974), 65.

33. Topping, "Overland Emigrants," 16.

34. Ibid., 16–18; Hunt, *Ghost Trails to California*, 64–67.

35. Faragher, *Women and Men on the Overland Trail*, 7; Unruh, *The Plains Across*, 342–56.

36. Stewart, *Ordeal by Hunger*, 220.

37. Unruh, *The Plains Across*, 341.

38. Topping, "Overland Emigrants," 18–24.

39. Ibid., 24, 28–29.

3 : Archaeology of the Murphy Cabin

1. See, for example, the sketch of the lake camp based on the account of survivor William Murphy in *History of Nevada County, California*, ed. Harry L. Wells (Oakland, Calif.: Thompson and West, 1880).

2. "Mary Murphy's Story," letter in Charles Covillaud file, Yuba County Library, Marysville, Calif.; quoted in Steed, *The Donner Party Rescue Site*, 13.

3. McGlashan, *History of the Donner Party*, 90.

4. Stewart, *Ordeal by Hunger*, 257–67.

5. Mrs. Murphy's name appears variously as Lavinia, Lavina, and Levina in written accounts.

6. Stewart, *Ordeal by Hunger*, 198.

7. Houghton, *Expedition of the Donner Party*, 109.

8. Ibid., 207–8.

9. Bryant, *What I Saw in California*, 263.

10. Nathaniel V. Jones, "The Journal of N. V. Jones with the Mormon Battalion," *Utah Historical Quarterly* 4 (1931): 19; Thomas Swords, *Report of a Journey from California by the South Pass to Fort Leavenworth in 1847*, report to the 30th U.S. Congress, 2d sess., House Executive Document 1, serial set 537, 1848; Memoirs of Matthew Caldwell, Adams Family Collection, MS 82, Marriott Library, University of Utah. (I am grateful to Kristin Johnson for making me aware of the Caldwell memoirs.)

11. Jones, "Journal," 19.

12. McGlashan, *History of the Donner Party*, 260.

13. Erwin G. Gudde, ed., *Bigler's Chronicle of the West* (Berkeley: University of California Press, 1962), 73.

14. John Markle Diary, 1849 (Manuscript on file at the Emigrant Museum, Donner Memorial State Park, Truckee, Calif.).

15. David Morris Potter, ed., *Trail to California: The Overland Journal of Vincent Geiger and Wakeman Bryarly* (New Haven: Yale University Press, 1962), 202.

16. I am grateful to Don Wiggins, a researcher of emigrant trails, who converted the original handwritten diary now in the Library of Congress into a typescript copy and provided me with this quote. The Oregon-California Trails Association plans to publish the diary in their Emigrant Trails Historical Studies Series.

17. *Truckee Republican*, May 7, 1872.

18. McGlashan, *History of the Donner Party*, 260–61.

19. M. Nona McGlashan and Betty McGlashan, eds., *From the Desk of Truckee's C. F. McGlashan* (Truckee, Calif.: Truckee-Donner Historical Society, 1986), 115; see also C. F. McGlashan, *The Location of Site of Breen Cabin* (Oakland, Calif.: privately printed, 1920), 7–8.

20. An earlier version of some of the material in this chapter was published in Hardesty, "The Archaeology of the Donner Party Tragedy"; the research was supported in part by National Geographic Society Grant Number 2814–84.

21. Michael B. Schiffer, *Formation Processes of the Archaeological Record* (Tucson: University of Arizona Press, 1987).

22. Susan Lindström, "An Archaeologically and Historically Based Rendition of the Murphy Cabin: Donner Memorial State Park" (Report prepared for Tahoe Sierra State Parks Association and Donner Memorial State Park, Truckee, Calif. 1986), 22.

23. Samples of the last foundation log, bottled by C. F. McGlashan in 1897, showed no signs of charring.

24. James M. Fife and Barbara Sutherland, "The Murphy Cabin Reconstruction Project" (Manuscript on file at the Emigrant Museum, Donner Memorial State Park, Truckee, Calif., 1983), 1.

25. Hardesty, "The Archaeology of the Donner Party Tragedy," 255.

26. Stewart, *Ordeal by Hunger*, 65.

27. McGlashan, *History of the Donner Party*, 259.

28. Louis A. Garavaglia and Charles G. Worman, *Firearms of the American West, 1803–1865* (Albuquerque: University of New Mexico Press, 1984), 41.

29. Ibid.

30. McGlashan, *History of the Donner Party*, 73; Stewart, *Ordeal by Hunger*, 99.

31. Paul R. Huey Jr., "A Possible Bristol-Made TD Tobacco Pipe Bowl from Johnson Hall," *Society for Historical Archaeology Newsletter* 25, no. 3 (1992): 5.

32. Letter from Richard Ahlborn, National Museum of American History, Smithsonian Institution, to Donald Hardesty, February 13, 1985.

33. Daniel Tyler, *A Concise History of the Mormon Battalion in the Mexican War* (Salt Lake City, 1881); see also Andrew Jensen, ed., *Historical Record*, vol. 8 (Salt Lake City: privately published, 1889), 928.

34. Murphy, "Across the Plains," as reprinted in Johnson, *Unfortunate Emigrants*, 282.

35. McGlashan, *History of the Donner Party*, 258.

36. Hardesty, "Archaeology of the Donner Party Tragedy," 264–65.

37. John Price, *Washoe Economy*, Nevada State Museum Anthropological Papers 6 (Carson City: Nevada State Museum, 1962).

38. Amy Dansie, "The Rye Patch Archeofauna," in *The Humboldt Project, Rye Patch Reservoir: Phase IV Archaeological Data Synthesis*, ed. Mary Rusco and Jonathan O. Davis, Nevada State Museum Archaeological Services Reports (Carson City: Nevada State Museum, 1982).

39. See, for example, Jerold M. Lowenstein, "Molecular Approaches to the Identification of Species," *American Scientist* 73 (1985): 541–47.

40. Letter from Jerold Lowenstein to Sheilagh Brooks, February 3, 1986.

41. Letter from Jerold Lowenstein to Sheilagh Brooks, February 3, 1988.

42. Wells, *History of Nevada County, California*.

43. Houghton, *The Expedition of the Donner Party*, 347.

44. Murphy, "Across the Plains," 23.

45. Houghton, *Expedition of the Donner Party*, 109.

46. Letter from Eliza P. Donner Houghton to C. F. McGlashan, May 25, 1879, Bancroft Library, McGlashan Collection, Box 1, Folder 28.

47. Letter from W. C. Graves to C. F. McGlashan, April 13, 1879, Bancroft Library, McGlashan Collection.

48. Potter, *Trail to California*, 201.

49. Joseph Warren Wood, "Journal of an Expedition to California, 1849–1852" (Manuscript on file at the Huntington Library, Pasadena, Calif.).

50. Charles R. Parke, "Journal of a Trip across the Plains from Illinois to California" [1849] (Manuscript on file at the Huntington Library, Pasadena, Calif.).

51. Potter, *Trail to California*, 201.

52. Terry Jordan and Matti Kaups, *The American Backwoods Frontier: An Ethnic and Ecological Interpretation* (Baltimore: Johns Hopkins University Press, 1989), 180, fig. 7.1B.

53. McGlashan, *History of the Donner Party*, 61.

54. Henry Glassie, *Pattern in the Material Folk Culture of the Eastern United States* (Philadelphia: University of Pennsylvania Press, 1968); Fred B. Kniffen and Henry Glassie, "Building in Wood in the Eastern United States: A Time-Space Perspective," *Geographical Review* 56 (1966): 40–66; Jordan and Kaups, *The American Backwoods Frontier*.

55. Jordan and Kaups, *The American Backwoods Frontier*, 209.

56. Ibid.

57. Ibid., 179–210.

58. McGlashan, *History of the Donner Party*, 61; Potter, *Trail to California*, 201.

59. McGlashan and McGlashan, *From the Desk of Truckee's C. F. McGlashan*, 115.

60. Harry L. Wells, ed., *History of Nevada County, California* (Oakland: Thompson and West, 1880).

61. Potter, *Trail to California*, 201.

62. Ibid.

63. Elliott Wigginton, *The Foxfire Book* (Garden City, N.J.: Doubleday/Anchor, 1972), 55.

4 : Archaeology of the Alder Creek Camp

Some of the material in this chapter was previously published in Hardesty and Lindström, *Archaeology of the Donner Family Camp*, and in Hardesty, "Donner Party Archaeology."

1. Letter from Leanna Donner App to C. F. McGlashan, April 1, 1879, 3, McGlashan Papers, Bancroft Library.
2. Stewart, *Ordeal by Hunger*, 84.
3. King, *Winter of Entrapment*, 46.
4. Quoted in Stewart, *Ordeal by Hunger*, 259.
5. Ibid., 260.
6. Quoted in McGlashan, *History of the Donner Party*, 91.
7. Quoted in King and Steed, "John Baptiste Trudeaux of the Donner Party," 168–69.
8. Quoted in Stewart, *Ordeal by Hunger*, 262.
9. Ibid., 267.
10. Ibid., 273.
11. Quoted in Morgan, *Overland in 1846*, 1:339.
12. Ibid., 357–58.
13. Ibid., 361.
14. Jones, "Journal," 19.
15. Tyler, *Mormon Battalion*, as cited in Jensen, *Historical Record*, 8:929.
16. Markle diary.
17. P. M. Weddell, "Location of the Donner Family Camp," *California Historical Society Quarterly* 24, no. 1 (March 1945): 75; McGlashan, *History of the Donner Party*, editors' notes to the 1947 reprint of the 1880 (2d) edition, xxxv.
18. Weddell, "Location of the Donner Family Camp," 75.
19. Ibid.
20. Ibid., 74.
21. See, for example, Harold Curran, *Fearful Crossing* (Reno: Great Basin Press, 1982); Charles Graydon, *Trail of the First Wagons over the Sierra Nevada* (Gerald, Mo.: Patrice Press, 1986); W. Turrentine Jackson, "Historical Survey of the Stampede Reservoir Area in the Little Truckee River Drainage District" (Report prepared for the National Park Service, San Francisco, 1967); Morgan, *Overland in 1846*; George R. Stewart, *The Opening of the California Trail* (Berkeley: University of California Press, 1953).
22. Charles Kelly and Dale Morgan, *Old Greenwood* (Georgetown, Calif.: Talisman Press, 1965).
23. Horace S. Foote, *Pen Pictures from the Garden of the World* (Chicago: Lewis Publishing Company, 1888), contains a narrative by Moses Schallenberger describing the ordeal.
24. Overton Johnson and William H. Winter, *Route across the Rocky Mountains, with a Description of Oregon and California* (Lafayette, Ind.: privately printed, 1846); Kelly and Morgan, *Old Greenwood*; Jacob R. Snyder, "The Diary of Jacob R. Snyder Written while Crossing the Plains to California in 1845," *Quarterly of the Society of California Pioneers* 8 (December 1931): 224–260.

25. Charles K. Graydon, "The Emigrant Trail in the Vicinity of the George Donner Campground" (Manuscript on file at the Tahoe National Forest Office, Nevada City, Calif., 1989), 2; Snyder, "Diary"; Markle diary.

26. *Sacramento Bee*, October 11, 1941, magazine section, 3.

27. McGlashan, *History of the Donner Party*, 63.

28. Quoted in King and Steed, "John Baptiste Trudeaux of the Donner Party," 172.

29. *Sacramento Bee*, October 11, 1941, magazine section, 3.

30. *Sierra Sun and Truckee Republican*, July 15, 1943, 1.

31. Curran, *Fearful Crossing*; Graydon, *Trail of the First Wagons*.

32. The letter, written by her husband, is in the McGlashan Collection, Bancroft Library, University of California, Berkeley.

33. The letter, written by her daughter, is in the McGlashan Collection at the Bancroft Library.

34. Stewart, *Ordeal by Hunger*, 84.

35. Quoted in Morgan, *Overland in 1846*, 1:339.

36. Houghton, *Expedition of the Donner Party*.

37. McGlashan, *History of the Donner Party*, 63; letter written by Eliza Donner Houghton, November 30, 1902, McGlashan Papers, Bancroft Library.

38. Morgan, *Overland in 1846*, 1:361.

39. Sidney B. Brinckerhoff, *Metal Uniform Insignia of the Frontier U.S. Army 1846–1902*, Arizona Historical Society Museum Monograph 3 (Tucson: Arizona Historical Society, 1972), 14.

40. Letter from Glenn Farris, California Department of Parks and Recreation, to Susan Lindström, March 29, 1991.

41. Morgan, *Overland in 1846*, 2:563.

42. Murphy, "Across the Plains," 26.

5 : Donner Party Baggage

1. Daniel E. Sutherland, *The Expansion of Everyday Life, 1860–1876* (New York: Harper and Row, 1990).

2. Thomas J. Schlereth, *Victorian America, Transformations in Everyday Life, 1876–1915* (New York: HarperCollins, 1991).

3. Unruh, *The Plains Across*.

4. Reprinted in Johnson, *Unfortunate Emigrants*, 265–266.

5. Michael A. Capps, "Wheels in the West: The Overland Wagon," *Overland Journal* 8, no. 4 (1990): 9.

6. Ibid.

7. Stewart, *The California Trail*, 119.

8. Unruh, *The Plains Across*.

9. King, *Winter of Entrapment*, 35–36.

10. Unruh, *The Plains Across*, 245.

11. Ibid., 251–52.

12. James F. Reed, "Narrative of the Sufferings of a Company of Emigrants in the Mountains of California, in the Winter of '46 and '47," *Springfield Illinois Journal*, December 9, 1847.

13. Stewart, *Ordeal by Hunger*, 284.

14. Ibid., 16.

15. The *Sacramento Bee*, April 11, 1927, reported that Donner party buff Charles E. Davis, who explored and marked the trail taken by the party, found what may have been the cache in the Great Salt Lake Desert in 1927.

16. Hawkins and Madsen, *Excavation of the Donner-Reed Wagons*.

17. Stewart, *Ordeal by Hunger*, 261.

18. Ibid., 193.

19. Fort Sutter Papers (1847), vol. 26, MSS 112–114.

20. Ibid., MS 110.

21. As reproduced in King, *Winter of Entrapment*, 99.

22. Ibid., 100.

23. Ibid.

24. Breen's sketch is reproduced in King, *Winter of Entrapment*, 214.

25. Bryant, *What I Saw in California*, 263.

26. See, for example, Potter, *Trail to California*; Parke, "Journal of a Trip across the Plains"; Wood, "Journal of an Expedition to California."

27. Quoted in Potter, *Trail to California*, 201.

28. McGlashan, *History of the Donner Party*, 258.

29. Ibid.

30. Ibid., 257–58.

31. Ibid., 258.

32. Helen McKearin and Kenneth W. Wilson, *American Bottles and Flasks and Their Ancestry* (New York: Crown, 1978).

33. Olive Jones and Catherine Sullivan, *The Parks Canada Glass Glossary* (Ottawa: Canadian Parks Service, 1989), 14.

34. Garavaglia and Worman, *Firearms of the American West*, 51.

35. Mentioned in Patrick Breen's diary entry for December 29, 1846, as reprinted in Stewart, *Ordeal by Hunger*, 260.

36. Melvin M. Johnson Jr. and Charles T. Haven, *Ammunition, Its History, Development and Use* (New York: William Morrow, 1943), 34.

37. Reprinted in Stewart, *Ordeal by Hunger*, 261.

38. C. P. Russell, *Guns on the Early Frontier* (Berkeley: University of California Press, 1957), 243.

39. Hawkins and Madsen, *Excavation of the Donner-Reed Wagons*, 87.

40. As quoted in Garavaglia and Worman, *Firearms of the American West*, 42.

41. McGlashan, *History of the Donner Party*, 259.

42. See, for example, Johnson and Haven, *Ammunition*, 26–28.

43. Sally C. Luscomb, *The Collector's Encyclopedia of Buttons* (New York: Crown, 1979), 17, 109.

44. Ibid., 163, 169; Elizabeth Hughes and Marion Lester, *The Big Book of Buttons* (Sedgewick, Maine: New Leaf Publishers, 1991), 785.

45. Hughes and Lester, *The Big Book of Buttons*, 203.

46. Lee Motz, "The Murphy Cabin Beads," in Hardesty, "Archaeology of the Murphy Cabin Site" (Report prepared for the National Geographic Society, Washington, D.C., 1985).

47. Lester Ross, "Bohemian Glass Beads: Late 19th-Century Temporal Markers" (Paper presented at the Society for Historical Archaeology Conference on Historical and Underwater Archaeology, Reno, Nev., 1988).

48. For example, Karlis Karklins and Roderick Sprague, *A Bibliography of Glass Trade Beads in North America* (Moscow, Idaho: South Fork Press, 1980); Karlis Karklins and Roderick Sprague, *A Bibliography of Glass Trade Beads in North America: First Supplement* (Ottawa: Promontory Press, 1987).

49. Related by Thornton, in Johnson, *Unfortunate Emigrants*, 50.

50. King, *Winter of Entrapment*, 61.

51. Stewart, *Ordeal by Hunger*, 263.

52. Huey, "A Possible Bristol-Made TD Tobacco Pipe Bowl," 5; Iain C. Walker, *Clay Tobacco Pipes, with Particular Reference to the Bristol Industry* (Ottawa: Parks Canada, 1977).

53. Henry C. Mercer, *Ancient Carpenters' Tools* (Doylestown, Pa.: Bucks County Historical Society, 1960), 200–201.

54. Albert Jerome Dickson, ed., *Covered Wagon Days* (1929; reprint, Lincoln: University of Nebraska Press, 1989); see also Michael A. Capps, "Wheels in the West."

55. Amos J. Loveday Jr., *The Rise and Decline of the Cut Nail Industry* (Westport, Conn.: Greenwood Press, 1983).

56. Capps, "Wheels in the West," 6; Stewart, *The California Trail*, 112; Mattes, *The Great Platte River Road*, 43.

6 : New Directions in Donner Party Research

1. Morgan, *Overland in 1846*, 2:715–16.

2. Donald K. Grayson, "Donner Party Deaths: A Demographic Assessment," *Journal of Anthropological Research* 46, no. 3 (1990): 223–42.

3. Ibid., 232–33.

4. For example, J. P. W. Rivers, "Women and Children Last: An Essay on Sex Discrimination in Disasters," *Disasters* 6 (1982): 256–67.

5. Donald K. Grayson, "Human Mortality in a Natural Disaster: The Willie Handcart Company," *Journal of Anthropological Research* 52, no. 2 (1996): 185–205.

6. Stewart, *Ordeal by Hunger*, 72.

7. For example, Weddell, "Location of the Donner Family Camp," 74.

Appendix One: Zooarchaeology of the Murphy Cabin Site

1. In Hardesty, "Archaeology of the Donner Party Tragedy," 246–68.

2. Thornton, *Oregon and California in 1848*, 20.

3. Hardesty, "Archaeology of the Donner Party Tragedy."

4. K. R. Gordon, "Molar Measurements as a Taxonomic Tool in *Ursus*," *Journal of Mammalogy* 58 (1977): 247–48; R. W. Graham, "Variability in the Size of North American Quaternary Black Bears (*Ursus americanus*) with the Description of a Fossil Black Bear from Bill Neff Cave, Virginia," in *Beamers, Bobwhites, and Blue-Points: Tributes to the Career of Paul W. Parmalee*, ed. R. Purdue, W. Klippel, and B. W.

Styles, Illinois State Museum Scientific Papers 23 (Springfield: Illinois State Museum, 1991), 237–50.

5. Graham, "Variability in the Size of North American Quaternary Black Bears," 1991.

6. Hardesty, "Archaeology of the Donner Party Tragedy."

Appendix Two: Ceramics from the Alder Creek Camp

1. George L. Miller and Robert R. Hunter Jr., "English Shell Edged Earthenware: Alias Leeds Ware, Alias Feather Edge," in *35th Annual Wedgwood International Seminar* (1990), 116.

2. Karen D. Boring, "A Survey of Ceramic Advertisements in the *National Daily Intelligencer, 1827–1837*" (Manuscript in the possession of George L. Miller, University of Delaware, 1973).

3. George L. Miller, "A Revised Set of CC Index Values for Classification and Economic Scaling of English Ceramics from 1787 to 1880," *Historical Archaeology* 25, no. 1 (1991): 8.

4. Andrew Lamb, "The Press and Labour's Response to Pottery-Making Machinery in the North Staffordshire Pottery Industry," *Journal of Ceramic History* 9 (1977): 2–4.

5. Ibid., 4–5.

6. Miller, "Classification," 17.

7. George L. Miller, "Origins of Josiah Wedgwood's 'Pearlware,'" *Northeast Historical Archaeology* 16 (1987): 83–88.

8. Geoffrey A. Godden, *Godden's Guide to Mason's China and the Ironstone Wares* (Woodbridge, Suffolk: Antique Collectors Club, 1980), 26–28; Miller, "Origins," 88–90.

9. Miller, "Origins."

Appendix Three: The Timing of Donner Party Deaths

1. D. K. Grayson, "Donner Party Deaths: A Demographic Assessment," *Journal of Anthropological Research* 46 (1990): 223–42.

2. R. L. Trivers, "Parental Investment and Sexual Selection," in *Sexual Selection and the Descent of Man*, ed. B. Campbell, 136–79 (Chicago: Aldine, 1972); W. Atmar, "On the Role of Males," *Animal Behavior* 41 (1991): 195–205.

3. H. W. Stoudt, A. Damon, and R. A. McFarland, "Heights and Weights of White Americans," *Human Biology* 32 (1960): 331–41.

4. A. U. Khan and J. Cataio, *Men and Women in Biological Perspective* (New York: Praeger, 1984).

5. U.S. Bureau of Justice Statistics, *Sourcebook of Criminal Justice Statistics—1991* (Washington, D.C.: U.S. Department of Justice, 1991).

6. R. Rohner, "Sex Differences in Aggression: Phylogenetic and Enculturation Perspectives," *Ethos* 4 (1976): 57–72.

7. U.S. Bureau of Labor Statistics, *Handbook of Labor Statistics*, Bureau of Labor Statistics Bulletin 2340 (Washington, D.C.: U.S. Department of Labor, 1989).

8. Stewart, *Ordeal by Hunger.*

9. Ibid.

10. Breen's diary is quoted in Stewart, *Ordeal by Hunger;* and King, *Winter of Entrapment.* Stewart's dates are in *Ordeal by Hunger.* I have spelled Mrs. Murphy's name "Lavina," following King, *Winter of Entrapment.* King gives Patrick Dolan's age as about thirty-five (p. 21), but I have retained Stewart's (1960) figure, forty years. Had King's figure been used, however, the outcome of my analysis would be the same.

11. Spearman's rho measures the tendency of ranked variables, in this case age and days-to-death, to covary: the higher the correlation coefficient (the maximum value is ± 1.0), the greater the tendency of the ranks to vary in concert. The p value indicates the probability that the calculated correlation coefficient could have occurred by chance. In this case, those odds are about 13/1,000.

12. Stewart, *Ordeal by Hunger.*

13. An outlier is a value that falls farther from a predicted value than can be explained by chance; standard deviations measure how far from the predicted value the actual value lies. In this case, the general relationship between age and days-to-death predicts that George Donner should have succumbed on about the 18th day. In fact, he died on the 102d day. The odds that this eighty-four-day difference can be explained by chance are about 8/1,000.

14. Grayson, "Donner Party Deaths."

15. Ibid.

LITERATURE CITED

Altrocchi, Julia Cooley
    1936   *Snow-Covered Wagons: A Pioneer Epic.* New York: Macmillan.
Atmar, W.
    1991   "On the Role of Males." *Animal Behavior* 41: 195–205.
Barry, Louise
    1972   *Beginning of the West: Annals of the Kansas Gateway to the American West, 1540–1854.* Topeka: Kansas State Historical Society.
Beck, Warren A., and Ynez D. Haase
    1989   *Historical Atlas of the American West.* Norman: University of Oklahoma Press.
Bibby, Geoffrey
    1956   *The Testimony of the Spade.* New York: A. A. Knopf.
Birney, Hoffman
    1934   *Grim Journey.* New York: Minton, Balch and Company.
Boring, Karen D,
    1973   "A Survey of Ceramic Advertisements in the *National Daily Intelligencer, 1827–1837.*" Manuscript in the possession of George L. Miller, 1973.
Brinckerhoff, Sidney B.
    1972   *Metal Uniform Insignia of the Frontier U.S. Army 1846–1902.* Museum Monograph 3. Tucson: Arizona Historical Society.
Bryant, Edwin
    1848   *What I Saw in California.* Philadelphia: D. Appleton.
Caldwell, Matthew
    n.d.   Memoirs of Matthew Caldwell. Adams Family Collection, MS 82, Marriott Library, University of Utah, Salt Lake City.
Capps, Michael A.
    1990   "Wheels in the West: The Overland Wagon." *Overland Journal* 8 (4): 2–11.
Curran, Harold
    1982   *Fearful Crossing.* Reno: Great Basin Press.
Dansie, Amy
    1982   "The Rye Patch Archeofauna." In *The Humboldt Project, Rye Patch Reservoir: Phase IV Archaeological Data Synthesis,* ed. Mary Rusco and Jonathan

O. Davis. Nevada State Museum Archaeological Services Report. Carson City: Nevada State Museum.

DeVoto, Bernard
1943 *Year of Decision, 1846*. Boston: Houghton Mifflin.

Dickson, Albert Jerome (editor)
1929 *Covered Wagon Days*. Reprint. Lincoln: University of Nebraska Press, 1989.

Faragher, John Mack
1979 *Women and Men on the Overland Trail*. New Haven: Yale University Press.

Fife, James M., and Barbara Sutherland
1983 "The Murphy Cabin Reconstruction Project." Manuscript on file at the Donner Memorial State Park, Truckee, Calif.

Fisher, Vardis
1943 *The Mothers: An American Saga of Courage*. New York: Vanguard Press.

Foote, Horace S.
1888 *Pen Pictures from the Garden of the World*. Chicago: Lewis Publishing Company.

Garavaglia, Louis A., and Charles G. Worman
1984 *Firearms of the American West, 1803–1865*. Albuquerque: University of New Mexico Press.

Glassie, Henry
1968 *Pattern in the Material Folk Culture of the Eastern United States*. Philadelphia: University of Pennsylvania Press.

Godden, Geoffrey A.
1980 *Godden's Guide to Mason's China and the Ironstone Wares*. Woodbridge, Suffolk: Antique Collectors Club.

Gordon, K. R.
1977 "Molar Measurements as a Taxonomic Tool in *Ursus*." *Journal of Mammalogy* 58: 247–48.

Graham, R. W.
1991 "Variability in the Size of North American Quaternary Black Bears (*Ursus americanus*) with the Description of a Fossil Black Bear from Bill Neff Cave, Virginia." In *Beamers, Bobwhites, and Blue-Points: Tributes to the Career of Paul W. Parmalee*, ed. R. Purdue, W. Klippel, and B. W. Styles, 237–50. Illinois State Museum Scientific Papers 23. Springfield, Ill.

Graydon, Charles
1986 *Trail of the First Wagons over the Sierra Nevada*. Gerald, Mo.: Patrice Press.
1989 "The Emigrant Trail in the Vicinity of the George Donner Campground." Manuscript on file at the Tahoe National Forest Office, Nevada City, Calif.

Grayson, Donald K.
1990 "Donner Party Deaths: A Demographic Assessment." *Journal of Anthropological Research* 46: 223–42.
1996 "Human Mortality in a Natural Disaster: The Willie Handcart Company." *Journal of Anthropological Research* 52 (2): 185–205.

Gudde, Erwin G. (editor)
1962 *Bigler's Chronicle of the West*. Berkeley: University of California Press.

Hardesty, Donald L.
   1985 "Archaeology of the Murphy Cabin Site." Report prepared for the National Geographic Society, Washington, D.C.
   1987 "Archaeology of the Donner Party Tragedy." *Nevada Historical Society Quarterly* 30: 246–68.
   1992 "Donner Party Archaeology." *Overland Journal* 10 (3): 18–26.
Hardesty, Donald L., and Susan Lindström
   1990 "Archaeology of the Donner Family Camp." Report prepared for the Tahoe National Forest, Nevada City, Calif.
Hawkins, Bruce, and David Madsen
   1990 *Excavation of the Donner-Reed Wagons.* Salt Lake City: University of Utah Press.
Hopkins, Sarah Winnemucca
   1883 *Life among the Piutes.* New York: G. P. Putnam's Sons.
Houghton, Eliza P. Donner
   1911 *The Expedition of the Donner Party and Its Tragic Fate.* Chicago: A. C. McClurg.
Huey, Paul R. Jr.
   1992 "A Possible Bristol-Made TD Tobacco Pipe Bowl from Johnson Hall." *Society for Historical Archaeology Newsletter* 25 (3): 5–6.
Hughes, Elizabeth, and Marion Lester
   1991 *The Big Book of Buttons.* Sedgewick, Maine: New Leaf Publishers.
Hunt, Thomas H.
   1974 *Ghost Trails to California.* New York: Weathervane Books.
Jackson, W. Turrentine
   1967 "Historical Survey of the Stampede Reservoir Area in the Little Truckee River Drainage District." Report prepared for the National Park Service, San Francisco.
Johnson, Kristin
   1996 *"Unfortunate Emigrants": Narratives of the Donner Party.* Logan: Utah State University Press.
Johnson, Melvin M. Jr., and Charles T. Haven
   1943 *Ammunition, Its History, Development and Use.* New York: William Morrow.
Johnson, Overton, and William H. Winter
   1846 *Route across the Rocky Mountains, with a Description of Oregon and California.* Lafayette, Ind.: privately printed. Reprint. Princeton: Princeton University Press, 1932.
Jones, Nathaniel V.
   1931 "The Journal of N. V. Jones with the Mormon Battalion." *Utah Historical Quarterly* 4 (1): 1–24.
Jones, Olive, and Catherine Sullivan
   1989 *The Parks Canada Glass Glossary.* Ottawa: Canadian Parks Service.
Jordan, Terry, and Matti Kaups
   1989 *The American Backwoods Frontier.* Baltimore: Johns Hopkins University Press.

Karklins, Karlis, and Roderick Sprague
   1980   A Bibliography of Glass Trade Beads in North America. Moscow, Idaho:
          South Fork Press.
   1987   A Bibliography of Glass Trade Beads in North America, First Supplement.
          Ottawa: Promontory Press.
Kelly, Charles, and Dale Morgan
   1965   Old Greenwood. Georgetown, Calif.: Talisman Press.
Kern, Edward, et al.
   n.d.   Fort Sutter Papers, vol. 26. Manuscripts on file at the Huntington Library,
          Pasadena, Calif.
Khan, A. U., and J. Cataio
   1984   Men and Women in Biological Perspective. New York: Praeger.
King, Joseph A.
   1992   Winter of Entrapment: A New Look at the Donner Party. Toronto: P. D.
          Meany. Rev. ed. Lafayette, Calif.: K&K Publications, 1994.
King, Joseph A., and Jack Steed
   1995   "John Baptiste Trudeaux of the Donner Party: Rascal or Hero?" California
          History 74 (2): 162–173.
Kniffen, Fred B., and Henry Glassie
   1966   "Building in Wood in the Eastern United States: A Time-Space Perspec-
          tive." Geographical Review 56: 40–66.
Lamb, Andrew
   1977   "The Press and Labour's Response to Pottery-Making Machinery in the
          North Staffordshire Pottery Industry." Journal of Ceramic History 9: 1–10.
Leone, Mark, and Parker Potter
   1987   Introduction to The Recovery of Mind: Historical Archaeology in the Eastern
          United States, ed. Mark Leone and Parker Potter, 1–22. Washington, D.C.:
          Smithsonian Institution Press.
Lindström, Susan
   1986   "An Archaeologically and Historically Based Rendition of the Murphy
          Cabin: Donner Memorial State Park." Report prepared for the Donner Me-
          morial State Park and Tahoe Sierra State Parks Association, Truckee, Calif.
Lingenfelter, Richard E.
   1986   Death Valley and the Amargosa, a Land of Illusion. Berkeley: University of
          California Press.
Lovejoy, Amos J.
   1983   The Rise and Decline of the Cut Nail Industry. Westport, Conn.: Greenwood
          Press.
Lowenstein, Jerold M.
   1985   "Molecular Approaches to the Identification of Species." American Scientist
          73: 541–47.
Lowenthal, David
   1985   The Past Is a Foreign Country. Cambridge: Cambridge University Press.
Luscomb, Sally C.
   1979   The Collector's Encyclopedia of Buttons. New York: Crown.

Maino, Jeanette Gould
  1987   *Left Hand Turn: A Story of the Donner Party Women.* Modesto, Calif.: privately printed.
Markle, John
  1849   Diary. Manuscript on file at the Emigrant Museum, Donner Memorial State Park, Truckee, Calif.
Mattes, Merrill
  1969   *The Great Platte River Road.* Lincoln: Nebraska State Historical Society.
McGlashan, C. F.
  1879   *History of the Donner Party.* Truckee, Calif.: Crowley and McGlashan. Rev. ed. San Francisco: A. L. Bancroft, 1880.
  1920   *The Location of Site of Breen Cabin.* Oakland, Calif.: privately printed.
McGlashan, M. Nona, and Betty H. McGlashan (editors)
  1986   *From the Desk of Truckee's C. F. McGlashan.* Truckee, Calif.: Truckee-Donner Historical Society.
McKearin, Helen, and Kenneth W. Wilson
  1978   *American Bottles and Flasks and Their Ancestry.* New York: Crown.
Mercer, Henry C.
  1960   *Ancient Carpenters Tools.* Doylestown, Pa.: Bucks County Historical Society.
Miller, George L.
  1987   "Origins of Josiah Wedgwood's 'Pearlware.'" *Northeast Historical Archaeology* 16: 83–95.
  1991   "A Revised Set of CC Index Values for Classification and Economic Scaling of English Ceramics from 1787 to 1880." *Historical Archaeology* 25 (1): 1–25.
Miller, George L., and Robert R. Hunter Jr.
  1990   "English Shell Edged Earthenware: Alias Leeds Ware, Alias Feather Edge." *Thirty-fifth Annual Wedgwood International Seminar,* 107–36.
Morgan, Dale L.
  1943   *The Humboldt.* New York: Farrar and Rinehart.
Morgan, Dale L. (editor)
  1963   *Overland in 1846: Diaries and Letters of the Oregon-California Trail.* 2 vols. Georgetown, Calif.: Talisman Press.
Motz, Lee
  1985   "The Murphy Cabin Beads." In "Archaeology of the Murphy Cabin Site," by Donald L. Hardesty. Report prepared for the National Geographic Society, Washington, D.C.
Murphy, Virginia Reed
  1891   "Across the Plains in the Donner Party (1846)." *Century Magazine* (July). Reprint. Olympic Valley, Calif.: Outbooks, 1977.
Parke, Charles R.
  1849   "Journal of a Trip across the Plains from Illinois to California." Manuscript on file at the Huntington Library, Pasadena, Calif.

Potter, David Morris (editor)
  1962   *Trail to California: The Overland Journal of Vincent Geiger and Wakeman
          Bryarly.* New Haven: Yale University Press.
Price, John
  1962   *Washoe Economy.* Nevada State Museum Anthropological Papers 6. Carson
          City: Nevada State Museum.
Reed, James Frazier
  1847   "Narrative of the Sufferings of a Company of Emigrants in the Mountains of
          California, in the Winter of '46 and '47." *Illinois Journal* (Springfield), De-
          cember 9, 1847.
Rivers, J. P. W.
  1982   "Women and Children Last: An Essay on Sex Discrimination in Disasters."
          Disasters 6: 256–67.
Robinson, Francis C.
  1966   *The Donner Party in Fiction.* University of Colorado Studies, Series in Lan-
          guage and Literature 10. Boulder: University of Colorado. 87–93.
Rohner, R.
  1976   "Sex Differences in Aggression: Phylogenetic and Enculturation Perspec-
          tives." *Ethos* 4: 57–72.
Ross, Lester
  1988   "Bohemian Glass Beads: Late 19th-Century Temporal Markers." Paper pre-
          sented at the Society for Historical Archaeology Conference on Historical
          and Underwater Archaeology, Reno, Nev.
Russell, C. P.
  1957   *Guns on the Early Frontier.* Berkeley: University of California Press.
Schiffer, Michael B.
  1987   *Formation Processes of the Archaeological Record.* Tucson: University of Ari-
          zona Press.
Schlereth, Thomas J.
  1991   *Victorian America, Transformations in Everyday Life, 1876–1915.* New York:
          HarperCollins.
Snyder, Jacob R.
  1931   "The Diary of Jacob R. Snyder Written while Crossing the Plains to Califor-
          nia in 1845." *Quarterly of the Society of California Pioneers* 8 (December):
          224–60.
Steed, Jack
  1993   *The Donner Party Rescue Site: Johnson's Ranch on Bear River.* Rev. and exp.
          ed. Sacramento: privately printed.
Stewart, George R.
  1936   *Ordeal by Hunger: The Story of the Donner Party.* Boston: Houghton Miff-
          lin. Rev. ed. Lincoln: University of Nebraska Press, 1960.
  1953   *The Opening of the California Trail.* Berkeley: University of California Press.
  1962   *The California Trail.* Lincoln: University of Nebraska Press.
Stoudt, H. W., A. Damon, and R. A. McFarland
  1960   "Heights and Weights of White Americans." *Human Biology* 32: 331–41.
Sutherland, Daniel E.
  1990   *The Expansion of Everyday Life, 1860–1876.* New York: Harper and Row.

Swords, Thomas

1848 *Report of a Journey from California by the South Pass to Fort Leavenworth in 1847.* Report to the 30th United States Congress, 2d sess., House Executive Document 1, serial set 537, 1848.

Thornton, J. Quinn

1849 *Oregon and California in 1848.* 2 vols. New York: Harper and Brothers. Reprint. Golden, Colo.: Outbooks, 1986.

Topping, Gary

1990 "Overland Emigrants, the California Trail, and the Hastings Cutoff." In *Excavation of the Donner-Reed Wagons,* Bruce Hawkins and David Madsen, 11–15. Salt Lake City: University of Utah Press.

Trivers, R. L.

1972 "Parental Investment and Sexual Selection." In *Sexual Selection and the Descent of Man,* ed. Bernard Campbell, 136–79. Chicago: Aldine.

Tyler, Daniel

1881 *A Concise History of the Mormon Battalion in the Mexican War* Salt Lake City, Utah. Reprint. Chicago: Rio Grande Press, 1964.

United States Bureau of Justice Statistics

1991 *Sourcebook of Criminal Justice Statistics—1991.* Washington, D.C.: United States Department of Justice.

United States Bureau of Labor Statistics

1991 *Handbook of Labor Statistics—1989.* Bureau of Labor Statistics Bulletin 2340. Washington, D.C.: United States Department of Labor.

Unruh, John D. Jr.

1979 *The Plains Across: The Overland Emigrants and the Trans-Mississippi West, 1840–1860.* Urbana: University of Illinois Press.

Walker, Iain C.

1977 *Clay Tobacco Pipes, with Particular Reference to the Bristol Industry.* Ottawa: Parks Canada.

Weddell, P. M.

1945 "Location of the Donner Family Camp." *California Historical Society Quarterly* 24 (1): 73–76.

Wells, Harry L. (editor)

1880 *History of Nevada County, California.* Oakland, Calif.: Thompson and West.

White, Richard

1991 *"It's Your Misfortune and None of My Own": A New History of the American West.* Norman: University of Oklahoma Press.

Whitman, Ruth

1985 *A Woman's Journey.* Cambridge, Mass.: Alice James Books.

Wigginton, Elliott

1972 *The Foxfire Book.* Garden City, N.J.: Doubleday/Anchor.

Wood, Joseph Warren

1849 "Journal of an Expedition to California, 1849–1852." Manuscript on file at the Huntington Library, Pasadena, Calif.

INDEX